World Book Myths & Legends Series

CELTIC
MYTHS & LEGENDS

AS TOLD BY PHILIP ARDAGH

ILLUSTRATED BY G. BARTON CHAPPLE

World Book, Inc.
a Scott Fetzer company
Chicago

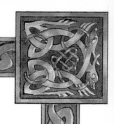

MYTH OR LEGEND?

Long before people could read or write, stories were passed on by word of mouth. Every time they were told, they changed a little, with a new character added here and a twist to the plot there. From these ever-changing tales, myths and legends were born.

WHAT IS A MYTH?

In early times, people developed stories to explain local customs and natural phenomena, including how the world and humanity developed. These myths were considered sacred and true. Most include superhuman beings with special powers.

WHAT IS A LEGEND?

A legend is very much like a myth. The difference is that a legend is often based on an event that really happened or a person who really existed in relatively recent times. King Arthur probably did exist but can't have done all the amazing things the Celts say he did.

WHO WERE THE CELTS?

The Celts originally occupied much of the British Isles and beyond. But after the Roman invasion of Britain in the first century A.D., the Celts were limited to Ireland, Wales, Cornwall, the Western Isles of Scotland, and Brittany–an area in northern France that was once part of the ancient country of Gaul. The Celts were called the Galli by the Romans, which is where the word *Gaelic* comes from, as in the Gaelic language spoken by many Celts. Although the origins of a particular myth or legend may come from one particular region, versions were told by Celts everywhere.

This map of the British Isles and the northern coastline of continental Europe shows the main areas where Celts lived after the Roman invasion of Britain in the first century A.D. The myths and legends in this book come from these Celtic regions.

WESTERN ISLES
OF SCOTLAND

IRELAND

WALES

CORNWALL

BRITTANY

One of the finest examples of Celtic metalwork is the Ardagh Chalice. This large silver cup is famous for its fine engraving and discs of red enamel. It is over 1,000 years old.

How Do We Know?

Many medieval records of Celtic myths survive to this day. In fact, written records about the legendary figure of King Arthur date back as far as the 9th century. Celtic myths became popular again in the 18th and early 19th centuries. This was when the Romantic movement–Romanticism– in art, music and literature brought new life to these imaginative, glorious tales of brave knights and beautiful ladies.

Note from the author

Myths and legends from different cultures were told in different ways. The purpose of this book is to tell new versions of these old Celtic stories, not to try to copy the way in which they were first told. I hope that you enjoy them and that this book will make you want to find out more about the Celts and their myths and legends.

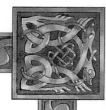

HEROES OF CELTIC MYTHS & LEGENDS

In this book you can find out about some of the best-known Celtic heroes and the fantastic myths and legends that have grown up around them. Here is a list of just some of the characters you will meet along the way. Alternative spellings of their names are shown in parentheses.

ARIANROD Mother of Llew. She was tricked by Gwydion into having his child.

ARTHUR King of the Britons. Arthur probably existed, but much earlier than the age of the knights in shining armor. Married to Guinevere.

BALOR Fomorian chieftain with an evil eye, who faced Lug in battle.

BLODEUWEDD Wife of Llew, made by Math from flowers woven together by magic.

CHANGELING A fairy child swapped with a human baby at birth. Usually lazy and clumsy.

CONCHOBAR (Conor) King of Ulster, hero and villain of many Irish myths.

CUCHULAIN (Cuchullain, Cuchulan) Ireland's greatest warrior of all time. Son of Lug and Dechtire.

CULAN Blacksmith and owner of the hound killed by Setanta.

DECHTIRE Sister of King Conchobar and mother of Cuchulain.

DEIRDRE Daughter of Fedlimid. It was prophesied that she would lead to Ireland's ruin.

EMER Daughter of Forgal the Wily, and wife of Cuchulain.

FAIRIES Another name for the Little People. They are especially common in Ireland, where they are called leprechauns.

4

FOMORS Hideous giants who invaded Ireland and faced the forces of Lug.

GUINEVERE King Arthur's queen. Loved by Sir Lancelot.

GWYDION Father of Llew and nephew of the ruler and sorcerer, Math.

LANCELOT Arthur's friend and greatest knight, secretly in love with Guinevere.

LITTLE PEOPLE Fairies, common in Celtic folklore. They are often fine sword makers and blacksmiths.

LLEW LLAW GYFFES (Lleu Law Gyffes) Welsh hero of many adventures. His mother, Arianrod, was tricked by Gwydion into having this child.

LUG (Lugh) Immortal High King of Ireland, Master of All Arts.

MATH Magician ruler of the Welsh realm of Gwynedd.

NAOISE Brother of Ardan and Ainle, the sons of Usnech; nephew to Conchobar; and lover of Deirdre.

NUADA King of the Tuatha Dé Danann, the rulers of all Ireland. He had a silver hand.

SETANTA Cuchulain's name before he killed the hound of Culan.

TUATHA DÉ DANANN The People of the goddess Danu, later seen as gods of Ireland themselves.

Shared Heroes

The best myths have often been absorbed into the myths of more than one hero, and experts believe that some heroes are the same person given a different name and background. For example, it has been suggested that the Welsh character Llew and the Irish character Lug are one and the same person—and that the town of Lyon in Brittany is named after him.

Appealing to an Audience

It is easy to see how this chopping and changing of stories came about. These stories were originally spoken, not written down. Every time a Celt retold a myth or legend, he or she would add local landmarks or events to make the story come alive to the people who were listening. Events in Brittany, for example, were changed if they were told in Scotland, Ireland, or Wales.

LLEW LLAW GYFFES THE BRIGHT ONE

In one of the most famous Welsh myths, Gwydion used magic to trick Arianrod into having his child. She never even knew their son existed until his fourth birthday, when Gwydion took him to meet her at her castle, Caer Arianrod, overlooking the sea.

"This is our son," said Gwydion, proudly pushing the boy forward into the light.

"You did a terrible thing," said Arianrod, "using magic to trick me like that." She looked at the boy. He was tall and strong for his age and had bright, burning eyes like his father's.

"What is his name?" she asked.

"He has no name," said Gwydion. "I thought it only right that you should be the one to choose it."

"So no one else shall name him?" asked Arianrod, still hurt by Gwydion's trickery.

"No one but you," Gwydion assured her. He hoped that meeting her child like this might melt Arianrod's heart and make her forgive him the wrongs he had done her in the past.

"Then the boy shall remain nameless forever!" cried Arianrod.

"Now go . . . and take the proof of your trickery with you."

Gwydion took their son's hand, turned, and strode toward the castle gates. Suddenly he stopped in his stride and looked back at Arianrod.

"I'll see you name the boy!" he swore. "Our son shall have a name!"

Down on the seashore Gwydion used his magic to trick Arianrod a second time. He wove a powerful spell, and magic hung heavy in the air like the sea mist all around them. When the mist lifted, both he and his son had taken on a different appearance, a moored boat had appeared on the water, and a shoemaker's tools and materials had been set up on the beach.

Soon news reached Arianrod that a cobbler and his apprentice had sailed into the cove. She sent one of her servants instructions to have them make her a pair of their finest shoes.

This was just as Gwydion had hoped. He made the most beautiful pair of shoes you can imagine . . . but deliberately made them just too big. The following day the servant returned and asked the cobbler to make her mistress another pair of shoes, the same as the first, only slightly smaller. This Gwydion did, but this time he deliberately made them too small. The next morning Arianrod came down to the cove herself to ask them to cut the leather to fit her soles.

There she witnessed the golden-haired apprentice fire an arrow into the air and strike a wren, the tiniest of birds and one of the hardest targets to hit.

Arianrod was impressed. "The bright one has a steady hand!" she smiled. "What is his name?"

"He had no name until this moment," said Gwydion, "but now you have given him one. He is the Bright One—the lion—with a Steady Hand," which, in the old language, was Llew Llaw Gyffes.

As he spoke, the boat disappeared from the water, the tools and materials disappeared from the beach, and Gwydion and his son were themselves once more.

Furious that she had been tricked once again, Arianrod flew into a rage, and Gwydion tried in vain to make her proud of their son.

"Llew is a fine name for a warrior, don't you agree?" he asked. "See how quickly he's already grown."

8

"But what warrior can fight without armor or weapons?" said Arianrod. "I swear that Llew shall have neither unless I give them to him, and that is something I shall never do."

With that, she started to climb up the winding path back to Caer Arianrod.

Llew grew into a hearty young man in half the time it would have taken any ordinary soul. He was handsome, strong, and a skilled horse rider, and it was soon time for him to learn how to use a sword.

So Gwydion and Llew found themselves once more at the huge gates of Caer Arianrod. And once again Gwydion used his magic to cast a spell to change their appearance.

This time they became a bard and his servant. Bards were proud wandering poets who entertained their audiences with epic poems about great feats of bravery. Gwydion and Llew were made very welcome by Arianrod and her court. They were well fed and given a grand chamber in which to spend the night.

While the rest of the castle was asleep, Gwydion climbed to the top of the highest tower of Caer Arianrod and stood facing the sea in the first glimmerings of morning light. A gentle breeze ruffled his hair as he muttered ancient words of illusion.

Arianrod awoke to the cries of her sentries, warning her that an enemy fleet had entered the bay and was about to lay siege to the castle. A soldier burst into Gwydion's chamber carrying a handful of weapons. He asked Gwydion and Llew to take up arms and help protect the castle, but Gwydion refused.

"This is not our fight," he said. "We are bards, not warriors. Leave us be."

When news of this response reached Arianrod, she knocked at their chamber door and entered.

"Your poems talked of brave deeds and heroic acts," she said. "Are they just words to you? Will you not live up to them and fight my enemy alongside me?"

6

"Very well," said Gwydion. "But give the boy some armor."
Soon a pair of Arianrod's maidens returned with armor, which
Arianrod buckled to the youth.

"Now give the boy weapons," said Gwydion, "and we shall prepare."
As soon as Arianrod heaped a pile of weapons into Llew's arms, all
the ships in the bay drifted away like the illusions that they really were,
and Gwydion and Llew were revealed as their true selves.

Arianrod was stunned. "Is there no end to your trickery?" she asked,
aghast. "Well, here's a curse that you cannot trick me into undoing!"
She strode across the stone floor to the chamber window and
threw the wooden shutters wide open.

"I swear by all things sacred that there is not, never was, and never
shall be a woman from any of the races in all the world who will
take Llew as her husband," she screamed, the wind carrying her
words across the sea.

Arianrod thought she had been clever with her curse. Her careful
wording had made sure that Gwydion could not raise the dead
to give his son a bride, nor wait until a girl grew into a woman
after the curse had been made.

"Is not, never was, and never shall be," were the words she had chosen,
and she felt sure they were the right ones. She was satisfied that no
woman could ever take Llew as her husband.

But Arianrod was mistaken. By being thorough and excluding all
women from any of the races in all the world, she had left Gwydion
with hope.

"What about a bride not born of *any* of the races . . . not born
of people?" he said. "This might be the way to break the curse!"

"You want me to marry a she-wolf?" asked his puzzled son.

"No," laughed Gwydion. "We will use magic to make you a wife!"

So Gwydion took Llew to Gwydion's uncle, the great magician
Math, who ruled the realm of Gwynedd from his mighty throne.
Gwydion told Math of the curse and his ideas for breaking it.

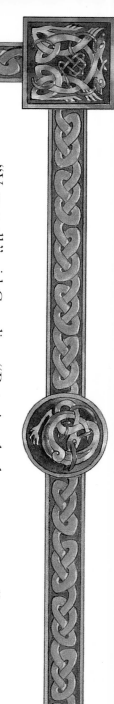

"I will give you a bride, Llew," Math said and told Gwydion and Llew to pick the blossoms of oak trees, the flowers of broom bushes, and the petals of the meadowsweet, and to bring them to him.

When this was done, Math wove them together with strong bonds of magic to create the most beautiful and graceful woman Llew had ever seen.

"I have never seen such beauty," he said in wonder. "She has the beauty of all Nature."

"She is to be called Blodeuwedd, or Flower Face," said Math.

"She will take you as her husband."

So now Llew was strong and handsome, had a proud name, was a great warrior with armor and weapons, and—after a magnificent wedding feast—was married to the beautiful Blodeuwedd.

Llew took Blodeuwedd to live in Mur Castell in the hills of Ardudwy—lands given to him by Math as a wedding gift—where he became a wise and much-loved ruler of his people.

But Llew's life was not all happiness. Later Blodeuwedd betrayed and killed him, but, once again, Math came to his rescue. He used his magic to bring one of the Celts' greatest heroes back to life.

LUG—THE MASTER OF MASTERS

Tara was the high seat of the Irish kings. Here King Nuada gathered the best of his people to form a council of war against the Fomors—the hideous giants from across the sea.

After all the others had gathered, a stranger arrived at the entrance to Tara. Though young and unscarred, he was dressed as a warrior king. He knocked on the gate.

"Who are you?" asked the gatekeeper. "What do you want?"

"I am Lug," said the stranger, "and I wish to join the council."

"Many seek entry, but very few are admitted," said the gatekeeper. "Only those who are the true masters of their craft may enter here."

"I'm a blacksmith," said Lug.

"Tara has a blacksmith," said the gatekeeper.

"I'm a carpenter," said Lug.

"Tara has a carpenter," replied the gatekeeper.

"I'm a poet and a storyteller," continued Lug.

"We already have the best within these walls," snapped the gatekeeper.

Lug tried healer, magician, musician . . . and each time, the gatekeeper told him that the master of such a craft was already inside Tara.

"You may already have a master for each of these crafts, but I am master of them all," said Lug. "Surely that gives me the right to enter?"

The gatekeeper heard a ring of truth in the newcomer's words. There was no boastfulness in the stranger's voice. Either he really was as masterful as he claimed, or at least he believed that he was.

"I shall speak with King Nuada and ask whether he grants you entry," said the gatekeeper.

When he entered the great hall and told the king about Lug and his claims at the gates of Tara, all those around him laughed.

"You bother the king with such obvious lies?" one grinned. "Send this imposter on his way."

But Nuada banged his fist on the arm of his throne, demanding silence. There was a time when the king had had no fist to bang. His hand had been cut off in the battle that made his people, the Tuatha Dé Danann, rulers of Ireland. Nuada had a hand made from silver, but now his hand was as good as new, thanks to the healing powers of one called Miach. Some had doubted the powers of Miach in the beginning, just as Lug was being doubted now.

"One as masterful as this Lug claims to be should have no trouble playing fidchell," commented the king. "Set up a board and pieces, and let's see how well he does against our best players."

So the board game, a bit like chess, was set up outside Tara, and Lug took up the challenge. He not only beat every man and woman he played, he beat them as they'd never been beaten before. He played with such amazing speed it was difficult to imagine when he found time to think. He even invented a move never used before.

On hearing the news of Lug's victory, the king came to meet him at the gates in person, led him inside, and sat him in the one unfilled seat on the council—that of the person with the greatest knowledge. Not everyone was happy with the way King Nuada welcomed this young newcomer. Who did Lug think he was? Ogma, the champion of Tara, decided to put him in his place. He stepped in front of Lug's seat, bent down and—with eyes bulging and muscles as hard as iron —pulled an enormous flagstone from the floor.

Some say that it had taken over 80 oxen to drag the stone into place, and now Ogma was rolling it across the courtyard and out of the gates of Tara.

"I wonder if the newcomer would put it back in place for me?" grinned Ogma, sweat pouring from his red face.

Lug said nothing. He knew that he was being tested–when all he wanted was to be accepted. He strode through the gates, and a moment later, to the complete and utter amazement of all those inside Tara, the huge flagstone was tossed over the wall and came crashing down in its original place, landing perfectly square in the hole it had left behind.

After that, Lug played them all such sweet music and sang such beautiful songs that the people of Tara had never felt so refreshed and ready to make plans for war. They gave Lug the title Samildánach, which means Master of All Arts.

Then King Nuada made an important decision. He decided that, because Lug was so gifted, Lug should lead the council of war. He also decided that because this was the job of a king, he should hand over the crown to Lug while the plans were laid.

This is how it came to be that Lug sat on the throne at Tara –with Nuada on his right in the seat of knowledge–when important strategies were made.

The planning continued. Days became weeks, and soon a year had passed. And still the hideous Fomorian giants had not come. Lug went back to the people of Manánann mac Lir. When the Fomors finally landed on Irish soil, Lug took his people with him to face them.

With so much careful planning and such strong magic, it seemed that the Tuatha Dé Danann would be victorious. Tara's magicians turned the trees and rocks of Ireland into warriors to fight the Fomors. Tara's cup bearers–those who served wine in the royal household–wove a spell that made the 12 rivers and 12 lakes of Ireland invisible to the enemy. This meant that no matter how thirsty the Fomors were, they could find no water in the land.

15

Magic spears were also used, which never missed their target.

Diancecht—whose son, Miach, had healed Nuada's severed hand—used his knowledge to heal all the warriors' wounds, except for those who had lost their heads. Each night the dead warriors were taken to a special spring by Diancecht and his handmaidens. Here the fallen were bathed, their injuries washed away, and they were brought back to life.

News of the secret of this magic spring finally reached a chief of the Fomorian army. Named Balor, he was one of its fiercest warriors, and by a quirk of fate, he was also Lug's own grandfather. Balor ordered his men to heap stones upon the source, where the water sprang from the earth. Soon they had built a huge cairn, and the healing waters were trapped deep underground. Now Balor felt ready for his army to meet his enemies face to face in battle.

As the Fomorian army gathered on the eastern side of the plain of Moytura, and the Tuatha Dé Danann gathered on the west side, there was unrest in the Danann ranks. News spread that the magic spring was gone, and their spirits fell. The Fomors were giants, and they were many. What chance did the Tuatha Dé Danann have against them?

Hearing that the troops were disheartened, Lug rode up and down the lines of soldiers offering words of encouragement. Catching sight of his glinting armor, one of the soldiers commented, "Strange how today the sun chooses to rise in the west instead of the east!"

Then the battle commenced. The Tuatha Dé Danann fought bravely, none more so than Queen Macha—wife of King Nuada—who fought at her husband's side. Nuada was killed by Balor, and Macha also perished. Soon the battlefield was piled high with bodies and running with blood. Many Irish chiefs died that day, but still the battle raged.

The hideous giant Balor had an evil eye. The eyelid was closed and kept in place by a special ring of brass. The ring was so heavy that it could only be lifted by four men. One glance from Balor's eye would kill whomever it fell upon. This made it a mighty weapon against enemies, but also a danger to friends.

Balor faced Lug now–grandfather against grandson. The Fomorian chief ordered his henchmen to his side.

"Lift the brass ring to free my eyelid so that I might gaze upon this little champion of the Tuatha Dé Danann," he roared.

Four of the Fomors stepped forward and began to lift the ring. But Lug was ready for them. He pulled out his sling shot and let loose a stone that hit the half-opened eye. The stone was a magic one, and it struck the giant's evil eye with such force that the eyeball was pushed through the back of Balor's skull and onto the battlefield. When it stopped spinning in the mud, the evil eye came to rest with its gaze upon a huge group of Fomorian warriors, who instantly dropped down dead.

Seizing the moment, Lug raised his sword and led his army through the break in the Fomors' line. Victory was theirs, and those Fomors who were not slain fled from Irish soil, never to return.

Lug ruled as an Irish High King for 40 years, though what became of him after that is shrouded in mystery. Some say he drowned. Others say that he is a god and will live forever.

DEIRDRE–A LIFE OF SORROW

This Irish myth tells the tragic tale of a woman called Deirdre and a prophecy that would lead to the downfall of all Ireland. This ancient story, which has been told and retold in many forms, also has strong links with the Celts of Scotland.

Conchobar, King of Ulster, was at a feast given by Fedlimid. With him were the Red Branch, his greatest warriors. During the festivities news reached the high table that Fedlimid's wife had given birth to their long-awaited child–a baby girl. There was much rejoicing. Then suddenly Cathbad the Druid rose from his seat and tried to speak above the noise.

"This is no cause for celebration," he bellowed, and because all those present knew that he had the gift of prophecy, they fell silent to hear his words.

"This is a terrible day for Ireland and for the Red Branch, for this tiny babe shall grow into a woman who shall lead to Ireland's ruin and the destruction of the Red Branch! She must be called Deirdre, which means 'troubler,'" he declared.

One of the Red Branch leapt to his feet and pulled his sword from its scabbard. "I say we slay the babe Deirdre now before she can do any harm!" he cried, and there were rumblings of agreement from his fellow warriors.

"Hold fast!" commanded the king. "We are guests of Fedlimid. We are here at his invitation. Would you have us slaughter the newly born daughter of our host?"

The warrior looked shamefaced and returned to his seat.

"I say we send Deirdre away to a place where she knows nothing of what has been prophesied here today; and then, when she is fully grown, I will take her as my wife. As queen she will love all Ireland. As my wife the Red Branch shall be her protectors. Why, then, would she wish them ill?" said Conchobar.

The assembled company cheered. This was an admirable solution from a wise king. Relieved that the king had spared his new-born daughter's life, but horrified by the druid's prophecy, Fedlimid gave Deirdre to Conchobar who took her in his arms.

Now the king sent the baby to be brought up in a small castle in the forest, where she was cared for by a nurse, a forester, and a woman called Levarcham. But only Levarcham knew who this child really was.

Deirdre had a happy childhood and grew into a caring and loving young woman, but the only man she ever saw was the forester.

One cold winter's day she sat staring out of the window onto the snow-covered ground.

"I wish I had a husband whose skin was as white as snow," she said.

Then a trickle of blood from a slaughtered calf came from under the door of a shed in the courtyard and stained the snow bright crimson.

"I wish I had a husband whose cheeks were as red as blood," she added.

A hungry raven swooped down at the sight of the blood and flew off in search of food.

"I wish I had a husband whose hair was as black as the raven's feathers," she finished.

Levarcham was distressed to see the girl she'd grown to think of as her own daughter looking so sad.

"I know a man who has snow-white skin, blood-red cheeks, and hair that's raven-black," she said. "His name is Naoise. He is one of the three sons of Usnech, and is the king's nephew."

Deirdre pleaded with Levarcham to meet this man. Against her better judgment, Levarcham gave in and invited Naoise to the castle in the forest. The two met and fell in love.

In time Naoise discovered that this fair maiden was Deirdre of the prophecy whom his uncle, King Conchobar, had pledged to marry.

"I can come and visit you here in the castle in the forest," he said, "but we can never be together."

"Why not?" said Deirdre. "Don't tell me that you don't have the same feelings for me as I for you. I know you do."

"Of course I do," cried Naoise, "but Conchobar has pledged to marry you, and he is our king."

"Then we shall go to a place, far from here, where he does not rule," protested Deirdre.

And so it came to be that Deirdre avoided the ever-watchful eye of Levarcham and fled with Naoise to Scotland, accompanied by Naoise's brothers, Ardan and Ainle, who traveled with them for protection.

Years passed, and Deirdre and Naoise were blissfully happy in Scotland in a place called Alba. But Conchobar still wanted to take Deirdre as his wife. He claimed that it was to protect all Ireland and the Red Branch against Cathbad's prophecy of ruin and destruction. But the truth was that Conchobar had heard reports of Deirdre's beauty and wanted her for himself. He had learned of her whereabouts and decided to send someone to bring the runaways home.

The king chose Fergus for the task because he was one of the most famed heroes of all Ireland. "Go in my name and bring Deirdre and my nephew Naoise back to Ulster," he commanded.

"I will not force them, since they have done no harm," said Fergus.

"I said nothing of force," said the king. "Offer them safe passage. Promise them that they are free to leave whenever they wish."

Fergus traveled with his sons to show that his intentions were honorable and that he meant no harm. But Deirdre would not trust him. He told them of the king's promise, but still she feared a trap.

21

"We should go, beloved," Naoise insisted. "Conchobar is my uncle, and he has given his word as a king."

Finally Deirdre agreed to travel back to Ireland to hear what Conchobar had to say. Ardan and Ainle were eager to go, too, for they missed the island of their birth.

As they were leaving, Deirdre began to sing a sorrowful song. This song later became known as "Farewell to Alba," for Deirdre was never to return to Scotland.

Back on Irish soil, Conchobar tricked Fergus into parting company from the others by inviting him to an important feast. Fergus could not refuse him. Without their protector, meanwhile, Deirdre, Naoise and his brothers, and the sons of Fergus were all made welcome at the hall of the Red Branch, home to the King of Ulster's finest warriors. They didn't suspect a trap until Levarcham—who, remember, had brought up Deirdre from a baby—came to warn them.

"Prepare to defend yourselves or flee this place!" she cried, but it was too late. Moments later the doors flew open, and Conchobar's men were upon them.

There are many stories about how well Deirdre's party fought against the Red Branch. The three sons of Usnech stood around her, protecting her with shield and spear, and each one killed over 300 of their enemies. But they were hopelessly outnumbered, and the king had another weapon—the magic of Cathbad the Druid. Cathbad cast a spell upon them, and they were defeated.

The sons of Usnech—Deirdre's beloved Naoise and his brothers Ardan and Ainle—were taken away and beheaded. Before the blade touched Naoise's neck, he raised his eyes to the heavens and swore his everlasting love for Deirdre.

When, later, Deirdre stumbled upon his open grave, she let down her hair and sang the saddest song ever sung on Irish soil. Throwing herself onto Naoise's body, Deirdre then gave him three kisses and died.

Hearing the news, King Conchobar was not displeased. He ordered that Deirdre be buried next to Naoise and that a wooden stake be hammered into each grave. "That way we can be sure that no magic can bring them back to life," he said.

Then he summoned Cathbad. "See, Deirdre is dead, yet Ireland does not lie in ruins and the Red Branch is as strong as ever!" he crowed. "Here's one prophecy of yours that won't be coming true, Druid!"

But Conchobar had spoken too soon. It was no longer an honor to be a member of the Red Branch. Many came to see them as a group of fighters who carried out orders without a thought for right or truth, and finally their numbers dwindled until they were no more.

Horrified by what the King of Ulster and his Red Branch had done, many of his subjects turned their backs on him and swore allegiance to another king. Now Irishman turned against Irishman. The prophecy had been fulfilled.

Meanwhile, the two wooden stakes driven into the graves of Deirdre and Naoise grew into a pair of yew trees. Their branches became entwined like the arms of lovers, embracing each other for eternity.

23

Arthur and the Sword in the Stone

Perhaps the best known of all Celtic heroes is King Arthur, the legendary king of the Britons. The Welsh and Cornish claimed him as their own, and in Brittany he was seen as a godlike figure.

When the mighty King Uther Pendragon died, there was no prince in his castle to take his place and to rule the Britons. It was not long before quarrels broke out about who should be the new king.

The head bishop ordered that all lords should come to the great church in the capital to attend Christmas Mass. When Mass was done, the bishop led them into the churchyard where, to everyone's amazement, there was an extraordinary sight to behold. There stood a huge stone. On that stone was an anvil, and sticking through the anvil into the stone, was a sword.

"Whoever pulls this sword from this stone and anvil is the rightful king of the Britons," said the bishop, though he did not say how the sword came to be there.

Every lord in attendance took his turn to try to pull out the sword, but it moved for no one.

Every New Year's Eve there was a special jousting tournament in the capital, and knights and their squires came from all over the land to prove their skills. One such knight, a true and loyal follower of the late King Uther Pendragon, was Sir Ector, who lived deep in the countryside. But news of the sword in the stone had not yet reached him.

This New Year's Eve the tournament was to be a special one for Sir Ector and his family. It was to be the first at which his son, Sir Kay, would fight as a knight. The third member of the party to attend the tournament was Arthur, whom Sir Ector had brought up as if he were his own flesh and blood. Arthur would act as Kay's squire, attending him, tending his horse, and looking after his armor and weapons.

On the morning they set off for the tournament, Sir Ector's wife and all the staff were lined up outside their castle to wish them Godspeed and a safe journey.

Kay's mother kissed him on both cheeks.

"Though winning is important, a knight's honor is more important still," she reminded him. "Fight fairly and be true."

"I will, Mother," Sir Kay beamed, climbing astride his horse.

"Be good, Arthur," she said, kissing him in turn, for she truly loved him as if he were her own son, which he assumed he was. "You'll make a fine squire for your brother, and it won't be long until you, too, are a knight."

Bursting with boyish pride, Arthur climbed upon his horse—less grand than Sir Kay's steed, admittedly, but one he loved dearly.

Then it was time to depart.

"This year we shall win great honors!" said Sir Ector. "I feel sure of it."

He gave his mount a tap with his spurs, and the three horses began the three-day ride to the New Year's Eve tournament.

On the first night of the journey, Sir Ector's party slept at the house of a friend who hadn't yet heard news of the sword in the stone. The talk that evening at the dinner table was of jousts, not of the extraordinary sword that would reveal the true king of the Britons.

The second night—just half a day's ride from the tournament —there was talk of little else at the tavern where Sir Ector, Sir Kay, and Arthur were staying. But they were so tired from their travels that they went straight to their rooms and to bed, and heard nothing of it.

26

Meanwhile in the tavern below, men from far and wide gossiped about the sword and the future king.

"Whoever he is, he will be a fine champion," said one, banging his drinking cup down on the oak table. "It will take enormous strength to pull that sword from its place."

The ale flowed, and the gossip continued through till morning.

So eager was Sir Kay to get to the tournament—for in previous years he had always been his father's squire and not a knight in his own right—that the small party set off at first light.

It was as they reached the outskirts of the capital, and the tower of the great church was in sight, that Sir Kay realized that his scabbard was empty. He'd left his sword back at their lodgings.

"A fine knight at a tournament I'll make without a sword!" he laughed. "I must return to the tavern to fetch it."

"I'll go," said Arthur. "You mustn't miss the start of the joust. Besides, I am your squire and should have made sure your sword was with you."

So Arthur hurried off back to the tavern, leaving Sir Ector and Sir Kay to enter the capital and to make their way to the jousting fields.

The sword, meanwhile, was nowhere to be found. What could he tell Kay? On his return he passed the churchyard to the great church and saw the sword sticking from the anvil and the stone. "What an extraordinary sight!" he thought.

Although ten knights were meant to guard it, none was at his post that day. Perhaps they were all at the joust. Perhaps magic was at work. Or perhaps it was fate that Kay had lost his sword in the first place and now young Arthur was able to seize this sword unchallenged.

"A strange place to leave a sword," he said to himself. "I'll borrow it, for Kay must have a weapon."

He strode across the churchyard and pulled the gleaming sword free from the stone with one clean stroke. It was as easy as pulling swords from a barrel of sand—something he sometimes did at home to treat old swords for rust.

"This is the finest sword I've ever seen," he mused, "an excellent substitute for Kay's missing weapon." Then he hurried to the joust and handed it to the young man he thought of as his brother.

Since Sir Kay and his father had parted company with Arthur, they'd heard stories about the sword in the stone from others on the road long before they reached the tournament. They'd even found time to stop in the churchyard and marvel at it.

This meant that the moment Arthur handed it to him, Kay recognized the sword from the stone. An incredible feeling of excitement and power pulsed through his body as he clutched the sword of the rightful king of the Britons.

He hurried to Sir Ector.

"Father!" he cried. "Father! I have the sword! I have the sword! I must be your rightful king!"

Sir Ector was amazed and took the mystical sword from his son's grasp. He studied the gold hilt and gleaming blade.

"This is indeed the sword from the churchyard," he spluttered, in absolute amazement. "How did you come by it, Kay? Did you pull it from the anvil and the stone?"

Somehow Kay felt less sure of himself now that the sword was no longer in his grasp. He felt like a knight at his first tournament. . . . He felt like a son who had lied to his father . . . like a brother who had betrayed his own brother. . . .

"No," said Sir Kay, his head bowed. "Arthur brought it to me."

"Arthur?" gasped Sir Ector. "We must go to him at once."

Back in the churchyard, Sir Ector ordered Arthur to replace the sword in the anvil and the stone. Arthur did so, and then Sir Ector and Sir Kay tried to pull it free. Try as they might, neither of them could pull the sword from the stone.

"Do as you did before, Arthur," said Sir Ector.

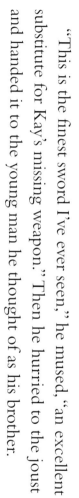

Arthur obeyed, and the sword slid as easily from the anvil and the stone as it had the first time—only this time it was before the witnesses of an ever-growing crowd.

Again Arthur replaced the sword, and again he pulled it free.

Sir Ector turned to the boy and looked him in the eye.

"Listen," he said, "for I have an important tale to tell."

Then Sir Ector told Arthur of his true beginnings.

"I am not your real father," he said. "As a baby you were brought to me by Merlin, magician and advisor to King Uther Pendragon, to be reared as my own. Now I realize that you must be the king's own flesh and blood. You are his son and heir."

"You are not my true family?" asked Arthur with sadness.

"We are all your family," said Sir Ector with a hug, "for you are Arthur, king of the Britons, and we are all your loyal subjects."

A year later Arthur was crowned king. He then set up court at Camelot and gathered together the Knights of the Round Table—the most famous knights in myth or legend.

The Death of King Arthur

The sword from the stone was a fine weapon, but King Arthur was soon to own the finest sword of them all. This sword was so great and so powerful that it had a name—Excalibur. It was given to Arthur by the Lady of the Lake, and it would be returned to her when King Arthur was betrayed and killed.

Arthur built a castle at Camelot. Inside the castle was a huge round table where Arthur and his knights sat when they gathered to meet. The Knights of the Round Table were the greatest knights the world has ever seen. And the greatest of them all was Sir Lancelot from Brittany.

King Arthur and his knights had many adventures and proved themselves honorable and chivalrous men. Their most glorious quest was for the Holy Grail—the cup from which Jesus Christ was said to have drunk at the Last Supper.

Arthur's queen was Guinevere, and they had married for love. This was against the advice of Merlin, the magician. Merlin—who had counseled King Uther Pendragon before Arthur—had become Arthur's most trusted advisor.

"Beautiful though Guinevere is," he warned, "she will bring much grief and sorrow to this land. But, if you love her, nothing I can say will make you change your mind."

For the magician knew that—deep in his heart—Sir Lancelot loved Guinevere, too, and that no good would come of this.

It was more usual, however, for the king to take Merlin's advice. One such occasion occurred when the magician came to him with news of a dreadful prophecy.

"Sire," he said, "a man born on this May Day will be your undoing."

"Then all boys of noble birth born on that day must be brought here to the castle, where they shall be brought up under my rules of chivalry," said the king.

Arthur would not accept that prophecies could be broken, so all the male babies in the land born on the day were put aboard a ship to sail to Camelot.

Suddenly a strange storm blew up out of nowhere. In the blinking of an eye, the calm waters were transformed into high, crashing waves, and the ship was smashed against the rocks. The ship was wrecked, and everyone on board perished—all, that is, except for a boy called Mordred, who was washed up on the shore. Mordred was found by a kindly man who brought him up as his own.

When Mordred reached the age of 14, he was taken to the court at Camelot and presented to King Arthur who—knowing nothing of his history—made him welcome. From that day on, while presenting himself as an honorable man, Mordred worked toward the king's undoing.

He decided that the best way to defeat King Arthur and the Knights of the Round Table was not by attacking them with an outside force, but by turning knight against knight from within.

Mordred knew that Sir Lancelot, the king's close friend, loved Guinevere, and he began to spread lies about the two of them meeting secretly. Over time he managed to convince 12 knights that they should kill Sir Lancelot for his disloyalty. Mordred planned to split the court of Camelot into two camps, for he knew that some knights would be against the king and some for him.

But when the 12 knights went to face Sir Lancelot, they were no match for him, and Lancelot survived.

Sadly, however, his friendship with Arthur did not. The king's mind had been poisoned by Mordred's rumors about Lancelot and Guinevere, and Arthur became so jealous that he ordered that his own wife be burned at the stake for loving another man.

This went against everything King Arthur stood for, but the king was still the king, and carrying out his orders, Sir Gaheris and Sir Gareth tied their queen to the stake and lit the flames. As the flames at her feet began to dance and lick the edge of her flowing robe, Sir Lancelot galloped into the courtyard and rescued her.

Mordred's plan was working. The Knights of the Round Table split into two groups, with brother fighting brother. Leaving Guinevere in his castle, Lancelot fled to Brittany. King Arthur rounded up a force and went after him. With the king out of the country, Mordred claimed the crown for himself. Now all he wanted was Guinevere as his bride.

Mordred lied to Guinevere, telling her that Arthur had died in battle and that he, Mordred, was now rightful king of the Britons and that she must be his queen.

When this news reached King Arthur, he hurried back to Britain and fought Mordred's forces. After much fighting, Mordred and Arthur agreed to hold a parley—the two men would meet to discuss a peaceful settlement, while those on the battlefield would stop fighting and tend to their wounded and dying.

At the parley Mordred admitted that he would never be able to claim the crown of all Britain while Arthur lived. He was no match for Arthur and the loyalty he brought out in his men. Arthur, on the other hand, knew that Mordred would always be a danger unless a lasting settlement could be reached, so he offered Mordred the dukedoms of Cornwall and Kent.

"And, when I die, the throne of the whole of Britain shall be yours," he added.

Mordred was delighted with these terms. He couldn't have hoped for more.

No one would question Mordred's right to the crown now that he had been named future king of the Britons by Arthur himself.

"Agreed!" he cried.

And that would have been the end of it, if a snake hadn't bitten the foot of one of Arthur's knights when the king returned to his camp on the battlefield. The knight—we know not whom—raised his sword to strike the adder, but this was taken as a signal for the fighting to restart now that the parley was over . . . and the battle resumed more ferociously than ever before.

The battle was so bloody that when evening came, there were only four people left standing out of many thousands. On one side was Mordred. On the other were King Arthur, Sir Lucan, and Sir Bedivere.

"Lend me your spear," the king ordered Sir Lucan. Arthur seized the spear and charged down the hill crying, "Traitor, your death day has come!"

Though Arthur found his target and ran the spear through the traitor, Mordred still managed to deal the king a fatal wound.

As Arthur lay dying, he was able to pull his sword, Excalibur, from its scabbard and hand it to Sir Bedivere.

"Take this to the lake," he instructed, "and throw it in. Then come back and tell me what you saw."

So Sir Bedivere took Excalibur, but could not bring himself to throw away the magical sword, so loved by the king. Instead, he hid it.

"It is done," he said, returning to the dying Arthur.

"And what did you see?" asked the king.

"Nothing but ripples on the water," said Sir Bedivere.

"Go and do as I asked," said Arthur.

Bedivere returned to the lake, uncovered the sword, but once again could not bring himself to throw it into the water.

He returned to the battlefield for the second time, and when asked by Arthur what he'd seen, he lied for the second time.

"I saw nothing but waves lapping the shore," he said.

King Arthur looked deep into Sir Bedivere's eyes.

"That is not truly spoken. Why would you betray me after years of such loyalty?"

Shamed and saddened, Sir Bedivere went to the lake a third time. This time he threw Excalibur as high and as far as he could.

It flew through the air in a graceful arc, and just before it hit the water, an arm and hand broke through the lake's surface to catch it. The hand brandished the sword three times and pulled it underwater.

When Bedivere told Arthur of this, the king smiled. Excalibur was with the Lady of the Lake once more. Then the dying king asked Bedivere to carry him to the water's edge where a funeral barge glided through the drifting mist. In it sat three silent women, draped in black. The dying king was lifted aboard the vessel, and Sir Bedivere bade him farewell. The barge set sail for the Isle of Avalon where Arthur lies to this day.

Some say that King Arthur is not dead but is sleeping. They call him the "once and future king." They say that, in Britain's greatest hour of need, he will awake and bring his people even greater victories.

CUCHULAIN—THE HOUND OF CULAN

Cuchulain, Ireland's mightiest warrior, was a handsome man. In battle, however, he took on a horrifying form. His skeleton swiveled inside his skin, one eye bulged and the other shrank, sparks poured from his mouth, and his body hissed with heat.

Conchobar, king of Ulster, had a beautiful sister called Dechtire. At a feast to mark Dechtire's marriage to Sualtam, a local chieftain, there was much celebration. When Dechtire's wine goblet was refilled, she didn't notice a May bug land in the liquid, and she swallowed it with a sip of wine. A moment later she found herself in a deep, deep sleep, and Lug, the hero of a bygone age, appeared to her.

"I was in that May bug," said Lug. "It will grow inside you and give you a son. Now come away with me and bring your maidens to attend you."

"But I cannot simply leave my own wedding feast," protested Dechtire. "I am Sualtam's now, and he is mine."

"No one will see you or your maidens," Lug promised, and he turned them into a flock of gleaming birds.

Nine months passed, and there had been no sight nor sound of Dechtire since she'd disappeared into thin air on her wedding day . . . that is, until a group of warriors out hunting one day followed a flock of the most extraordinary birds they'd ever seen. The flock led them to the place of the gods.

Night was falling, and the hunters were greeted by a richly dressed man who invited them to his palace, offering them food and shelter.

The hunters ate well and had nothing but praise for their mysterious host. But their sleep that night was interrupted by the cries of a new-born babe.

The following morning their host greeted them once more, but this time they saw him for who he really was. It was Lug, and in his arms was a shining baby boy.

"This is my son," he said, "mothered by Dechtire. Take mother, son, and their attending maidens back to Ulster. There the boy must be raised as a warrior."

So Dechtire was taken back to Ulster where her husband Sualtam was overjoyed to be reunited with his bride and was happy to raise the boy as his own. They called him Setanta.

From the earliest age Setanta showed remarkable skill at everything he did. There was no doubt that he was a son of Lug.

When Setanta was just 7 years old, he ran away to the court of his uncle, King Conchobar. There he was taught by Ulster's seven greatest heroes and poets—all deeply honored to be his teacher.

By the time Setanta was 12, he was stronger than most men, and loved to play hurley—a stick and ball game played between two teams. One day Culan the blacksmith prepared a great feast at his hall for the king and his finest warriors, and Conchobar wanted Setanta to accompany him.

"But I'm in the middle of a game!" the boy called out, as the king's party came to a halt at the edge of the field. He gave the ball such a "THWACK" with his stick that the opposing team scattered to avoid its path. "I will join you there, uncle," he said.

"Very well," agreed the king, and he and his warriors went on to Culan's hall.

Soon the feast was underway, and Culan the blacksmith put his hound at the gates to stand guard while he entertained his king.

In all the merriment Conchobar had completely forgotten that Setanta was yet to arrive and that he was not known to the dog. . . .

When the boy had finished the game of hurley–in which his team was, as always, victorious–he made his way to the great hall. The vicious, slavering guard dog attacked him at the gates. Fortunately for Setanta, he was not only very strong and very brave, but was also quick-thinking. He threw the hurley ball at the beast's mouth, and it became lodged in the dog's throat.

He then grabbed the startled creature by its hind legs and threw it against the wall.

"This child is truly the son of Lug," gasped Culan, "but there was no better guard dog than this hound. What protection can I offer now?"

Setanta heard the anger in his voice.

"I shall be your guard dog until a pup can be raised to take this one's place," he announced.

And, from that moment on, Setanta became known as Cuchulain, which means the Hound of Culan.

When Cuchulain was first given weapons and a chariot, he went off at once to face the three sons of Nechtan. These three warriors had been terrorizing the innocent people of Ulster with their evil ways and powerful magic, and many a brave man had been slaughtered trying to rid the island of them.

But Cuchulain returned victorious. He was a changed man –he would never be the same again. Now he challenged every warrior he met to mortal combat, and people everywhere came to fear him.

Finally he was caught by a group of women who tossed him into a barrel of water to cool his fighting spirit . . . a spirit so strong that the hoops of the barrel melted. In a second barrel he caused the water to bubble and boil, so they plunged him into a third. This final ducking was enough to bring Cuchulain to his senses.

After that, Cuchulain decided that it was time to take a wife. There was only one woman for him. And that was Emer, the daughter of Forgal the Wily. Wily means crafty and cunning, and Forgal was certainly that. When he discovered Cuchulain's interest in his daughter —and her interest in him—he sent the young hero on a quest.

Cuchulain was to visit Skye, one of the Western Isles of Scotland, where the island's queen, the warrior Scathac, would teach him how to become invincible. What Emer's wily father didn't tell the eager young Cuchulain was that Queen Scathac hated strangers and would surely kill him.

But Forgal had underestimated Cuchulain, who was, after all, the son of Lug. He made his way across the Scottish highlands, fighting beasts, fording rivers, and crossing a magic bridge that spanned a bottomless gorge, until he came upon Queen Scathac and took her by surprise. She was impressed by his skills.

"It is rare to find one who can catch me unawares," she said, and when he told her of the reason for his quest, the Scottish warrior queen agreed to teach Cuchulain all she knew.

With this knowledge Cuchulain returned to Ireland to claim Emer as his wife. It was then that he discovered that her father was not true to his word. Forgal had sent out his forces against him. But Cuchulain had little to worry about. He defeated them with ease, and when Forgal fled, he and Emer became husband and wife.

Perhaps Cuchulain's finest hour came in the battle called the Tain bo Cuailgne—the Cattle Raid of Cuailgne—when Queen Maeve of Connaught tried to seize a bull belonging to an Ulster chieftain.

This was a prize animal of great importance, so Maeve sent Fergus and his warriors to steal it. Once loyal to King Conchobar, Fergus had turned against him after the king's men had murdered Fergus's sons as they tried to protect doomed Deirdre from the prophecy.

Queen Maeve was sure that she would triumph over her enemies, because the warriors of Ulster were suffering from a terrible curse.

In times of trouble their bodies became weakened for a while, and they couldn't fight properly.

But Maeve hadn't reckoned on Cuchulain....

No curse could weaken him, and he was ready to fight. His skeleton swiveled inside his skin, one eye grew huge and the other shrank, sparks poured from his mouth, his body hissed with heat, and blood spurted from his head, filling the air with a thin red haze.

Some could not even bear to look at him in this state and simply turned and fled. Those who faced him were killed by the hundreds every day of the battle.

So many men died that a deal had to be struck. Cuchulain agreed to face one champion each day. But day after day he defeated the enemy. Queen Maeve, meanwhile, managed to capture the bull, but by then King Conchobar and his warriors had regained their strength, and Maeve and her forces were driven out of Ulster.

Cuchulain–the Hound of Culan–had many other adventures. He was finally slain up against a standing stone he'd bound himself to so that he would die on his feet. There was no greater warrior than this.

41

THE CHANGELING OF GREEN KNOLL

Ireland is a place of magic and home to the Little People. If you catch one, he has to tell you where he's hidden his pot of gold. But Scotland has its Little People, too, as this Celtic myth from the Western Isles reveals.

T he Green Knoll stood on a small island, near a cluster of cottages huddled together as protection against the cold winds of the Atlantic Ocean. It was a round and smooth grassy hill, and did not look as if it had been made by the hand of God. Some people said that it was a vast burrow—a burial chamber for an ancient people. Others said that it was home to the Little People—fairies who were rarely seen, but who made mischief in the village in the light of a full moon.

Many had tried to find an entrance into the Green Knoll, but without success. No villagers had dared to try digging their way in, because, whatever this strange hill was, there was a strong sense of magic about it. And no people in their right mind interfere with magic they do not understand.

Like the dwarfs of the Norse countries, these fairies were said to be skilled blacksmiths and fine weapon makers. They could beat beautiful swords, shields, and spears out of the hot metal on their anvils. Some villagers swore they heard a muffled clanging coming from deep within the heart of the hill. Others said it was simply the sounds–blown across the hill by the wind –of their local blacksmith, Iain, at work in his smithy.

43

Iain was a hard-working man. He had hoped that his son would be his apprentice and work alongside him, one day taking over the smithy as his own. But the boy had always been lazy. Instead of helping his father, he lay in bed, all day and every day, eating and drinking. That was all he ever seemed to do–eat and drink. But however much he ate and drank, he always wanted more and stayed as thin as a fire poker.

Soon rumors began to spread around the village that the boy wasn't a human child at all, but a changeling. A changeling is a fairy child, swapped with a human child soon after birth. He, or she, looks like a normal child but does not behave like one. There is something not quite right about a changeling, and now even Iain was beginning to suspect that this boy might not be his son at all.

"But how can I be sure?" he said one night, seated with his friends around a table in a farmer's barn. "For, if this is not my son, the Little People must have him, and I must find a way of rescuing him."

"I've heard that these changelings lead many lives," said the farmer.

"They may look like children, but they are hundreds of years old."

"I've heard that, too," said the farmer's wife. "And I've also heard that they like nothing more than to see something truly extraordinary—something they haven't seen in all their years."

"But how does that help me?" asked Iain the blacksmith.

"Because it is said that, on seeing such an extraordinary sight, a changeling cannot help but give himself away by crying out in amazement in his true voice," explained the woman.

"But what fantastic things can we show him here on our small island?" sighed Iain.

Just then the door blew open, and framed against the night sky stood an old man.

"Simple things can be made to seem extraordinary," he said. "The next time your son demands a drink, here is what you must do. . . ."

And the blacksmith and his friends listened with wide-eyed amazement.

44

Later that day the boy demanded a drink.

A moment later, following the old man's instructions, the blacksmith came into the boy's bedroom with half an eggshell filled with water in each hand.

Although eggshells are as light as light can be, and they hold very little water, the blacksmith pretended that they were as heavy as his anvil and that he had to drag himself across the room for the weight of them. He placed them at the boy's bedside with a groan and wiped his brow, looking exhausted.

The boy laughed. "In all the hundreds of years I've lived, I've never seen such an extraordinary sight as that!" he squealed in delight and, unaware that he had been tricked into giving himself away as a changeling, promptly demanded supper.

Now it was time for Iain the blacksmith to put the next part of the old man's plan into action, to rid himself of this changeling.

He began to build a large fire by the boy's bed.

"What are you doing, father?" he asked.

"You'll soon see," said the blacksmith, and when the fire was roaring hot, he snatched the boy and threw him toward the flames.

Before he had time to reach the fire, the changeling flew up into the air and smashed his way through the roof and out of the house forever.

Iain hurried to find the old man who was staying in the local inn.

"I've proved that the thing I brought up as my son is of fairy birth," he said. "But how will I ever get my true son back? How can I ever hope to find him?"

"He is inside the Green Knoll," said the man who, as well as being very old, was very wise. "But the only way in or out is on the night of a full moon when a great door appears in its side . . . a door that disappears at dawn."

"But it's a full moon tonight!" cried Iain.

"Which is why you must act quickly," said the old man.

Once again, he told the blacksmith exactly what to do.

45

Shivering with fear as well as cold, Iain the blacksmith made his way around the Green Knoll, bathed in silvery moonlight. And there, sure enough, was a huge door.

He reached out his hand and placed it on this magical entrance, which seemed to be made out of moonlight itself and was as cold as silver to the touch. It swung open. Clutching a Bible in one hand, and keeping a firm hold on a rooster hidden under his coat in the other—just as the old man had instructed—he took one last gulp of night air and then stepped into the blackness.

Now the frightened blacksmith was inside the hill, walking down a tunnel toward a warm orange glow that came from the very heart of the Green Knoll.

As he drew nearer, he could hear the familiar "CLANK," "CLANK" of skilled hands at work with a hammer and anvil, beating hot metal into shape. He found himself in a great hallway. There, scurrying around on the stone floor, and each of them no higher than his knee, were hoards of Little People. They paid no attention to him, for they were busy working the bellows of a fire and fetching metal and tools to an anvil at which a human boy—towering above them —was hard at work.

Iain gasped out loud, for here was his true son.

The Little People heard the blacksmith's gasp and turned, as one, to face him.

"Be gone and we will not harm you," their leader squealed. "If you stay and dawn comes, you, too, will be prisoner when the doorway melts away with the moonlight!"

"I'm not afraid of you," said Iain bravely, holding the Bible out in front of him for protection.

What the Little People didn't know was that Iain had also let the rooster out from under his coat. On seeing the warm glow of the fire where the irons were being heated, the bird thought this was the first sign of dawn and began to crow a rooster's greeting to the sun.

The Little People were thrown into a panic—just as the old man had intended as part of his plan for Iain to rescue his son.

They thought that it really was dawn, which meant that the doorway would close, shutting some of the Little People—who were off mischief-making—out of the Green Knoll until the next full moon. In the commotion Iain grabbed his son with one hand and, still clutching the Bible in the other, dashed for the exit.

By the time the Little People realized they'd been tricked by a confused rooster, the blacksmith was safely back in his smithy. And his son was safely back in the world of humans where he belonged.

MYTHS AND LEGENDS RESOURCES

Here is just a sampling of other resources to look for. These resources on myths and legends are broken down into groups. Enjoy!

GENERAL MYTHOLOGY

The Children's Dictionary of Mythology *edited by David Leeming* (Franklin Watts, 1999). This volume is a dictionary of terms, names, and places in the mythology of various cultures around the world.

Creation Read-aloud Stories from Many Lands *retold by Ann Pilling* (Candlewick Press, 1997). This is a collection of sixteen stories retold in an easy style and presented in three general groups: beginnings, warmth and light, and animals.

The Crystal Pool: Myths and Legends of the World *by Geraldine McCaughrean* (Margaret K. McElderry Books, 1998). Twenty-eight myths and legends from around the world comprise this book. They include the Chinese legend "The Alchemist" and the Celtic legend "Culloch and the Big Pig."

Encyclopedia Mythica
http://www.pantheon.org/areas/mythology/
From this page of the *Encyclopedia Mythica* site you can select from any of five countries to have the mythology of that area displayed.

A Family Treasury of Myths from Around the World *retold by Viviane Koenig* (Abrams, 1998). This collection of ten stories includes myths from Egypt, Africa, Greece, and other places around the world.

Goddesses, Heroes and Shamans: The Young People's Guide to World Mythology *edited by Cynthia O'Neill and others* (Kingfisher, 1994). This book introduces the reader to over five hundred mythological characters from around the world.

Gods, Goddesses and Monsters: An Encyclopedia of World Mythology *retold by Sheila Keenan* (Scholastic, 2000). This beautifully illustrated book discusses the characters and themes of the myths of peoples from Asia to Africa, to North and South America.

The Golden Hoard: Myths and Legends of the World *retold by Geraldine McCaughrean* (Margaret K. McElderry Books, 1995). This book contains twenty-two myths and legends that are exciting, adventurous, magical, and poetic.

The Illustrated Book of Myths: Tales and Legends of the World *retold by Neil Philips* (Dorling Kindersley, 1995). This beautifully illustrated collection brings together many of the most popular of the Greek and Roman, Norse, Celtic, Egyptian, Native American, African, and Indian myths.

Kids Zone: Myths and Fables from Around the World
http://www.afroam.org/children/myths/myths.html
Just click on your choice of the sixteen stories listed, and it will appear in full text.

Legends http://www.planetozkids.com/oban/legends.htm
From this Web page you can get the full text of any of the many listings.

Mythical Birds and Beasts from Many Lands *retold by Margaret Mayo* (Dutton, 1996). This book is a collection of stories that illustrate the special powers of birds and beasts that have become a part of folklore around the world.

Mythology *by Neil Philip* (Alfred A. Knopf, 1999). This superbly illustrated volume from the "Eyewitness Books" series surveys the treatment of such topics as gods and goddesses, the heavens, creation, the elements, and evil as expressed in various mythologies around the world.

Mythology *CD-ROM for Mac and Windows* (Thomas S. Klise, 1996). Educational games and puzzles, a glossary, and a testing section are all part of this CD introduction to Greek and Roman mythology.

Myths and Legends *by Neil Philip* (DK Publishing, 1999). More than fifty myths and legends from around the world are explained through works of art, text, and annotation by one of the world's foremost experts on mythology and folklore.

The New York Public Library Amazing Mythology: A Book of Answers for Kids *by Brendan January* (John Wiley, 2000). Over two hundred questions and answers introduce myths from many ancient cultures, including Egyptian, Greek, Roman, Celtic, Norse, and Native American.

Plays from Mythology: Grades 4-6 *by L.E. McCullough* (Smith and Kraus, 1998). Twelve original plays are included, each with suggestions for staging and costumes.

Sources for Mythology
http://www.best.com/~atta/mythsrcs.html
In addition to defining mythology and distinguishing it from legend and folklore, this Web site lists primary sources for myths from many regions of the world, as well as magazines, dictionaries, and other resources relating to mythology.

Sun, Moon and Stars *retold by Mary Hoffman* (Dutton, 1998). More than twenty myths and legends from around the world, all explaining what was seen in the sky, make up this exquisitely illustrated book.

AFRICAN

African Gods and their Associates
http://www3.sympatico.ca/untangle/africang.html
This Web page gives you a list of the African gods with links to further information about them.

African Myths
http://www.cybercomm.net/~grandpa/africanmyths.html
Full text of several tales from the Kenya, Hausa, Ashanti, and Nyanja tribes are included in this Web site.

Anansi and the Talking Melon *retold by Eric A. Kimmel* (Holiday House, 1994). Anansi, a legendary character from Africa, tricks Elephant and some other animals into thinking that the melon in which he is hiding can talk.

Children's Stories from Africa 4 *Video recordings* (VHS) (Monterey Home Video, 1997). Among the African Legends on this page: "How the Hare Got His Long Legs," "How the Porcupine Got His Quills," "The Brave Sititunga," and "The Greedy Spider."

The Hero with an African Face: Mythic Wisdom of Traditional Africa *by Clyde W. Ford* (Bantam, 2000). "The Hero with an African Face" is only one of the several stories included in this book, which also includes a map of the peoples and myths of Africa and a pronunciation guide for African words.

Kings, Gods and Spirits from African Mythology *retold by Jan Knappert* (Peter Bedrick Books, 1993). This illustrated collection contains myths and legends of the peoples of Africa.

Legends of Africa *by Mwizenge Tembo* (Metro Books, 1996). This indexed and illustrated volume is from the "Myths of the World" series.

Myths and Legends *retold by O. B. Duane* (Brockhampton Press, 1998). Duane has vividly retold some of the most gripping African tales.

CELTIC

Celtic Myths *retold by Sam McBratney* (Peter Bedrick, 1997). This collection of fifteen illustrated stories draws from English, Irish, Scottish, and Welsh folklore.

Excalibur *retold by Hudson Talbott* (Books of Wonder, 1996). In this illustrated story from the legends of King Arthur, Arthur receives his magical sword, Excalibur

Irish Fairy Tales and Legends *retold by Una Leavy* (Robert Rinehart, 1996). Cuchulainn, Deirdre, and Fionn Mac Cumhail are only three of the legendary characters you will meet in this volume.

Irish Myths and Legends
http://www.mc.maricopa.edu/users/shoemaker/Celtic/index.html
This Web site is for those more serious in their study of Irish myths and legends.

King Arthur *by Rosalind Kerven* (DK Publishing, 1998). This book from the "Eyewitness Classic" series is a retelling of the boy who was fated to be the "Once and Future King." It includes illustrated notes to explain the historical background of the story.

Robin Hood and His Merry Men *retold by Jane Louise Curry* (Margaret K. McElderry, 1994). This collection contains seven short stories of the legendary hero Robin Hood, who lived with his band of followers in Sherwood Forest.

The World of King Arthur and his Court: People, Places, Legend and Love *by Kevin Crossley-Holland* (Dutton, 1998). The author combines legend, anecdote, fact, and speculation to help answer some of the questions regarding King Arthur and his chivalrous world.

CHINESE

Asian Mythology *by Rachel Storm* (Lorenz, 2000). Included in this volume are myths and legends of China.

Chinese Culture
http://chineseculture.about.com/culture/chineseculture/msub82.htm
Use this Web page as a starting point for further exploration about Chinese myths and legends.

Chinese Mythology *by Anne Birrell* (Johns Hopkins, 1999). This comprehensive introduction to Chinese mythology will meet the needs of the more serious and the general reader

Chinese Myths and Legends *retold by O. B. Duane and others* (Brockhampton Press, 1998). Introductory notes by the author give further explanation of the thirty-eight stories included in this illustrated volume.

Dragons and Demons *by Stewart Ross* (Cooper Beech, 1998). Included in this collection of myths and legends from Asia are the Chinese myths "Chang Lung the Dragon" and "The Ugly Scholar."

Dragons, Gods and Spirits from Chinese Mythology *retold by Tao Tao Liu Sanders* (Peter Bedrick Books, 1994). The stories in this book include ancient myths about nature, the gods, and creation as well as religious legends.

Fa Mulan: The Story of a Woman Warrior *retold by Robert D. San Souci* (Hyperion, 1998). Artists Jean and Mou-Sien Tseng illustrate this Chinese legend of a young heroine who is courageous, selfless, and wise.

Land of the Dragon: Chinese Myth *by Tony Allan* (Time-Life, 1999). This volume from the "Myth and Mankind" series includes many of China's myths as well as examination of the myth and its historical roots.

Selected Chinese Myths and Fantasies
http://www.chinavista.com/experience/story/story.html
From this Web site and its links you will find several Chinese myths that are enjoyed by children as well as the history of Chinese mythology.

EGYPTIAN

Egyptian Gods and Goddesses *by Henry Barker* (Grosset and Dunlap, 1999). In this book designed for the young reader, religious beliefs of ancient Egypt are discussed, as well as their gods and goddesses.

Egyptian Mythology A-Z: A Young Reader's Companion *by Pat Remler* (Facts on File, 2000). Alphabetically arranged, this resource defines words relating to Egyptian mythology.

Egyptian Myths *retold by Jacqueline Morley* (Peter Bedrick Books, 1999). Legends of the pharaohs, myths about creation, and the search for the secret of all knowledge, make up this illustrated book.

The Gods and Goddesses of Ancient Egypt *by Leonard Everett Fisher* (Holiday House, 1997). This artist/writer describes thirteen of the most important Egyptian gods.

Gods and Myths of Ancient Egypt *by Mary Barnett* (Regency House, 1996). Beautiful color photographs are used to further explain the text in this summary of Egyptian mythology.

Gods and Pharaohs from Egyptian Mythology *retold by Geraldine Harris* (Peter Bedrick Books, 1992). The author gives some background information about the Ancient Egyptians and then retells more than twenty of their myths.

Myth Man's Egyptian Homework Help
http://egyptmyth.com/
Cool Facts and Fun for Kids and *Egyptian Myth Encyclopedia* are only two of the many wonderful links this page will lead you to.

Myths and Civilizations of the Ancient Egyptians *by Sarah Quie* (Peter Bedrick Books, 1998). The author intersperses Egypt's myths with a history of its civilization in this illustrated volume.

The Secret Name of Ra *retold by Anne Rowe* (Rigby Interactive Library, 1996). In this Egyptian myth, Isis tricks Ra into revealing his secret name so that she and her husband Osiris can become rulers of the earth.

Tales from Ancient Egypt *retold by George Hart* (Hoopoe Books, 1994). The seven tales in this collection include stories of animals, of Isis and Horus, of a sailor lost on a magic island, and of pharaohs and their magicians.

Who's Who in Egyptian Mythology *by Anthony S. Mercatante* (Scarecrow Press, 1995). The author has compiled a concise, easy-to-use dictionary of ancient Egyptian deities.

GREEK

Alita and the Queen: A Tale of Ancient Greece *by Priscilla Galloway* (Annick Press, 1995). This made-up story, which is based on Homer's epic poem, *The Odyssey*, reads like a novel.

Cupid and Psyche *retold by M. Charlotte Craft* (Morrow Junior Books, 1996). This classic love story from Greek mythology will appeal to young and old.

Gods and Goddesses *by John Malam* (Peter Bedrick Books, 1999). This volume is packed with information about the important gods and goddesses of ancient Greece, including Zeus, Hera, Athena, and Hades.

Greek and Roman Mythology *by Dan Nardo* (Lucent, 1998). The author examines the historical development of Greco-Roman mythology, its heroes, and its influence on the history of Western civilization.

NORSE

Beowulf *by Welwyn Wilton Katz* (Groundwood, 2000). The illustrations in this classic legend are based on the art of the Vikings.

Favorite Norse Myths *retold by Mary Pope Osborne* (Scholastic, 1996). These fourteen tales of Norse gods, goddesses, and giants are based on the oldest written sources of Norse mythology; *Prose Edda* and *Poetic Edda*.

The Giant King *by Rosalind Kerven* (NTC Publishing Group, 1998). Photos of artifacts from the Viking Age illustrate these two stories that are rooted in Norse mythology.

Gods and Heroes from Viking Mythology *by Brian Branston* (Peter Bedrick Books, 1994). This illustrated volume tells the stories of Thor, Balder, King Gylfi, and other Nordic gods and goddesses

Handbook of Norse Mythology *by John Lindow* (Ambcc, 2001). For the advanced reader, this handbook covers the tales, their literary and oral sources, includes an A-to-Z of the key mythological figures, concepts and events, and so much more.

Kids Domain Fact File
http://www.kidsdomain.co.uk/teachers/resources/fact_file_viking_gods_and_goddesses.html
This child-centered Web page is a dictionary of Viking gods and goddesses.

Myths and Civilization of the Vikings *by Hazel Martell* (Peter Bedrick, 1998). Each of the nine stories in this book is followed by a non-fiction spread with information about Viking society.

Norse Mythology: The Myths and Legends of the Nordic Gods *retold by Arthur Cotterell* (Lorenz Books, 2000). This encyclopedia of the Nordic peoples' myths and legends is generously illustrated with fine art paintings of the classic stories.

Odins' Family: Myths of the Vikings *retold by Neil Philip* (Orchard Books, 1996). This collection of stories of Odin, the All-father, and the other Viking gods Thor, Tyr, Frigg, and Loer is full of excitement that encompasses both tragedy and comedy.

Stolen Thunder: A Norse Myth *retold by Shirley Climo* (Houghton Mifflin, 1994). This story, beautifully illustrated by Alexander Koshkin, retells the Norse myth about the god of Thunder and the recovery of his magic hammer Mjolnir, from the Frost Giany, Thrym.

Guide for Using D'Aulaires' Book of Greek Myths in the Classroom *by Cynthia Ross* (Teacher Created Materials, 1993). This reproducible book includes sample plans, author information, vocabulary-building ideas, cross-curricular activities, quizzes, and many ideas for extending this classic work.

Hercules *by Robert Burleigh* (Harcourt Brace, 1999). Watercolor and color pencil illustrations help to tell the story of Hercules's final labor in which he went back to the underworld and brought back the three-headed dog, Cerberus.

Medusa *by Deborah Nourse Lattimire* (Joanna Cotler Books, 2000). The author/illustrator of this book re-creates the tragedy of one of the best-known Greek myths, the tale of the beautiful Medussa whose conceit causes a curse to be placed on her.

The Myths and Legends of Ancient Greece
CD-ROM for Mac and Windows (Clearvue, 1996). This CD conveys the heroic ideals and spirit of Greek mythology as it follows ten of the best-known myths.

Mythweb http://www.mythweb.com/
This Web page provides links to Greek gods, heroes, an encyclopedia of mythology, and teacher resources.

Pegasus, the Flying Horse *retold by Jane Yolen* (Dutton, 1998). This Greek myth tells of how Bellerophon, with the help of Athena, tames the winged horse Pegasus and conquers the monstrous Chimaera.

The Race of the Golden Apples *retold by Claire Martin* (Dial, 1991). Caldecott Medal winners Leo and Diane Dillon have illustrated this myth of Atalanta, the beautiful Greek princess.

The Random House Book of Greek Myths *by Joan D. Vinge* (Random House, 1999). The author retells some of the famous Greek myths about gods, goddesses, humans, heroes, and monsters, explaining the background of the tales and why these tales have survived.

The Robber Baby: Stories from the Greek Myths *retold by Anne Rockwell* (Greenwillow Books, 1994). Anne Rockwell, a well-known name in children's literature, has put together a superbly retold collection of myths that will be enjoyed by readers of all ages.

NORTH AMERICAN

Buffalo Dance: A Blackfoot Legend *retold by Nancy Van Laan* (Little, Brown and Company, 1993). This illustrated version of the Native North American legend tells of the ritual performed before the buffalo hunt.

The Favorite Uncle Remus *by Joel Chandler Harris* (Houghton Mifflin, 1948). This classic work of literature is a collection of stories about Brer Rabbit, Brer Fox, Brer Tarrypin, and others that were told to the author as he grew up in the South.

Iktomi Loses his Eyes: A Plains Indian Story *retold by Paul Goble* (Orchard Books, 1999). The legendary character Iktomi finds himself in a predicament after losing his eyes when he misuses a magical trick.

The Legend of John Henry *retold by Terry Small* (Doubleday, 1994). This African American legendary character, a steel driver on the railroad, pits his strength and speed against the new steam engine hammer that is putting men out of jobs.

The Legend of the White Buffalo Woman *retold by Paul Goble* (National Geographic Society, 1998). This Native American Plains legend tells the story of the White Buffalo Woman who gave her people the Sacred Calf Pipe so that people would pray and commune with the Great Spirit.

Myths and Legends for American Indian Youth http://www.kstrom.net/isk/stories/myths.html Stories from Native Americans across the United States are included in these pages.

Snail Girl Brings Water: a Navajo Story *retold by Geri Keams* (Rising Moon, 1998). This retelling of a traditional Navajo re-creation myth explains how water came to earth.

The Woman Who Fell from the Sky: The Iroquois Story of Creation *retold by John Bierhirst* (William Morrow, 1993). This myth describes how the creation of the world was begun by a woman who fell down to earth from the sky country, and how it was finished by her two sons.

SOUTH AMERICAN (INCLUDING CENTRAL AMERICAN)

Gods and Goddesses of the Ancient Maya *by Leonard Everett Fisher* (Holiday House, 1999). With text and illustration inspired by the art, glyphs, and sculpture of the ancient Maya, this artist and author describes twelve of the most important Maya gods.

How Music Came to the World: An Ancient Mexican Myth *retold by Hal Ober* (Houghton Mifflin, 1994). This illustrated book, which includes author notes and a pronunciation guide, is an Aztec pourquoi story that explains how music came to the world.

Llama and the Great Flood *retold by Ellen Alexander* (Thomas Y. Crowell, 1989). In this illustrated retelling of the Peruvian myth about the Great Flood, a llama warns his master of the coming destruction and leads him and his family to refuge on a high peak in the Andes.

The Legend of the Poinsettia *retold by Tomie dePaola* (G. P. Putnam's Sons, 1994). This beautifully illustrated Mexican legend tells of how the poinsettia came to be when a young girl offered her gift to the Christ child.

Lost Realms of Gold: South American Myth *edited by Tony Allan* (Time-Life Books, 2000). This volume, which captures the South American mythmakers' fascination with magic, includes the tale of the first Inca who built the city of Cuzco, as well as the story of the sky people who discovered the rain forest.

People of Corn: A Mayan Story *retold by Mary-Joan Gerson* (Little, Brown, 1995). In this richly illustrated creation story, the gods first try and fail, then try and fail again before they finally succeed.

Tales from the Rain Forest: Myths and Legends from the Amazonian Indians of Brazil *retold by Mercedes Dorson* (Ecco Press, 1997). Ten stories from this region include "The Origin of Rain" and "How the Stars Came to Be."

WHO'S WHO IN MYTHS AND LEGENDS

This is a cumulative listing of some important characters found in all eight volumes of the *World Book Myths and Legends* series.

A

Aegir (EE jihr), also called Hler, was the god of the sea and the husband of Ran in Norse myths. He was lord of the undersea world where drowned sailors spent their days.

Amma (ahm mah) was the creator of the world in the myths of the Dogon people of Africa. Mother Earth was his wife, and Water and Light were his children. Amma also created the people of the world.

Amun (AH muhn), later Amun-Ra, became the king of gods in later Egyptian myths. Still later he was seen as another form of Ra.

Anubis (uh NOO bihs) in ancient Egypt was the god of the dead and helper to Osiris. He had the head of a jackal.

Ao (ow) was a giant turtle in a Chinese myth. He saved the life of Kui.

Aphrodite (af ruh DY tee) in ancient Greece was the goddess of love. She was known for her beauty. The Romans called her Venus.

Arianrod (air YAN rohd) in Welsh legends was the mother of the hero Llew.

Arthur (AHR thur) in ancient Britain was the king of the Britons. He probably was a real person who ruled long before the age of knights in armor. His queen was Guinevere.

Athena (uh THEE nuh) in ancient Greece was the goddess of war. The Romans called her Minerva.

Atum (AH tuhm) was the creator god of ancient Egypt and the father of Shu and Tefnut. He later became Ra-Atum.

B

Babe (bayb) in North American myths was the big blue ox owned by Paul Bunyan.

Balder (BAWL dur) was the god of light in Norse myths. He was the most handsome of all gods and was Frigga's favorite son.

Balor (BAL awr) was an ancient chieftain in Celtic myths who had an evil eye. He fought Lug, the High King of Ireland.

Ban Hu (bahn hoo) was the dog god in a myth that tells how the Year of the Dog in the Chinese calendar got its name.

Bastet (BAS teht), sometimes Bast (bast) in ancient Egypt was the mother goddess. She was often shown as a cat. Bastet was the daughter of Ra and the sister of Hathor and Sekhmet.

Bellerophon (buh LEHR uh fahn) in ancient Greek myths was a hero who captured and rode the winged horse, Pegasus.

Blodeuwedd was the wife of Llew in Welsh legends. She was made of flowers woven together by magic.

Botoque (boh toh kay) in Kayapó myths was the boy who first ate cooked meat and told people about fire.

Brer Rabbit (brair RAB iht) was a clever trickster rabbit in North American myths.

C

Chameleon (kuh MEEL yuhn) in a Yoruba myth of Africa was a messenger sent to trick the god Olokun and teach him a lesson.

Conchobar (KAHN koh bahr), also called Conor, was the king of Ulster. He was a villain in many Irish myths.

Coyote (ky OH tee) was an evil god in myths of the Maidu and some other Native American people.

Crow (kroh) in Inuit myths was the wise bird who brought daylight to the Inuit people.

Cuchulain (koo KUHL ihn), also Cuchullain or Cuchulan, in Irish myths was Ireland's greatest warrior of all time. He was the son of Lug and Dechtire.

D

Culan (KOO luhn) in Irish myths was a blacksmith. His hounds was killed by Setanta, who later became Cuchulain.

Davy Crockett (DAY vee KRAHK iht) was a real person. He is remembered as an American frontier hero who died in battle and also in legends as a great hunter and woodsman.

Dechtire (DEHK teer) in Irish myths was the sister of King Conchobar and mother of Cuchulain.

Deirdre (DAIR dray) in Irish myths was the daughter of Fedlimid. She refused to wed Conchobar. It was said that she would lead to Ireland's ruin.

Di Jun (dee joon) was god of the Eastern Sky in Chinese myths. He lived in a giant mulberry tree.

Di Zang Wang (dee zahng wahng) in Chinese myths was a Buddhist monk who was given that name when he became the lord of the underworld. His helper was Yan Wang, god of the dead.

Dionysus (dy uh NY suhs) was the god of wine in ancient Greek myths. He carried a staff wrapped in vines.

Dolapo was the wife of Kigbo in a Yoruba myth of Africa.

E

Eight Immortals (ihm MAWR tuhlz) in Chinese myths were eight ordinary human beings whose good deeds led them to truth and enlightenment. The Eight Immortals were godlike heroes. They had special powers to help people.

El Niño (ehl NEEN yoh) in Inca myths was the ruler of the wind, the weather, and the ocean and its creatures.

Emer (AYV ur) in Irish myths was the daughter of Forgal the Wily and wife of Cuchulain.

F

Fafnir (FAHV nihr) in Norse myths was a son of Heidmar. He killed his father for his treasure, sent his brother Regin away, and turned himself into a dragon.

Frey (fray), also called Freyr, was the god of summer in Norse myths. His chariot was pulled by a huge wild boar.

Freya (FRAY uh) was the goddess of beauty and love in Norse myths. Her chariot was pulled by two large cats.

Frigga (FRIHG uh), also called Frigg, in Norse myths was the wife of Odin and mother of many gods. She was the most powerful goddess in Asgard.

Frog was an animal prince in an Alur myth of Africa. He and his brother, Lizard, competed for the right to inherit the throne of their father.

Fu Xi (foo shee) in a Chinese myth was a boy who, with his sister Nü Wa, freed the Thunder God and was rewarded. His name means Gourd Boy.

G

Gaunab was Death, who took on a human form in a Khoi myth of Africa. Tsui'goab fought with Gaunab to save his people.

Geb (gehb) in ancient Egypt was the Earth itself. All plants and trees grew from his back. He was the brother and husband of Nut and the father of the gods Osiris, Isis, Seth, and Nephthys.

Glooscap (glohs kap) was a brave and cunning god in the myths of Algonquian Native American people. He was a trickster who sometimes got tricked.

Guinevere (GWIHN uh vihr) in British and Welsh legends was King Arthur's queen, who was also loved by Sir Lancelot.

Gwydion (GWIHD ih uhn) in Welsh legends was the father of Llew and the nephew of the magician and ruler, Math.

H

Hades (HAY deez) in ancient Greece was the god of the dead. Hades was also called Pluto (PLOO toh). The Romans called him Dis.

Hairy Man was a frightening monster in African American folk tales.

Harpy (HAHRP ee) was one of the hideous winged women in Greek myths. The hero Jason and his Argonauts freed King Phineas from the harpies' power.

Hathor (HATH awr) was worshiped in the form of a cow in ancient Egypt, but she also appeared as an angry lioness. She was the daughter of Ra and the sister of Bastet and Sekhmet.

Heimdall (HAYM dahl) was the god in Norse myths who guarded the rainbow bridge joining Asgard, the home of the gods, to other worlds.

Hel (hehl), also called Hela, was the goddess of death in Norse myths. The lower half of her body was like a rotting corpse. Hel was Loki's daughter.

Helen (HEHL uhn), called Helen of Troy, was a real person in ancient Greece. According to legend, she was known as the most beautiful woman in the world. Her capture by Paris led to the Trojan War.

Heng E (huhng ay), sometimes called Chang E, was a woman in Chinese myths who became the moon goddess. She was the wife of Yi the Archer.

Hera (HEHR uh) in ancient Greece was the queen of heaven and the wife of Zeus. The Romans called her Juno.

Heracles (HEHR uh kleez) in ancient Greek myths was a hero of great strength. He was the son of Zeus. He had to complete twelve tremendous tasks in order to become one of the gods. The Romans called him Hercules.

Hermes (HUR meez) was the messenger of the gods in Greek myths. He wore winged sandals. The Romans called him Mercury.

Hoder (HOO dur) was Balder's twin brother in Norse myths. He was blind. It was said that after a mighty battle he and Balder would be born again.

Hoenir (HAY nihr), also called Honir, was a god in Norse myths. In some early myths, he is said to be Odin's brother.

Horus (HAWR uhs) in ancient Egypt was the son of Isis and Osiris. He was often shown with the head of a falcon. Horus fought Seth to rule Egypt.

Hreidmar (HRAYD mahr) was a dwarf king in Norse myths who held Odin for a huge pile of treasure. His sons were Otter, Fafnir, and Regin.

Hyrrokkin (HEER rahk kihn) in Norse myths was a terrifying female giant who rode an enormous wolf using poisonous snakes for reins.

I

Irin-Mage (eereen mah geh) in Tupinambá myths was the only person to be saved when the creator, Monan, destroyed the other humans. Irin-Mage became the ancestor of all people living today.

J

Jade Emperor (jayd EHM puhr uhr) in Buddhist myths of China was the chief god in Heaven.

Jason (JAY suhn) was a hero in Greek myths. His ship was the Argo, and the men who sailed with him on his adventures were called the Argonauts.

Johnny Appleseed (AP uhl seed) was a real person, John Chapman. He is remembered in legends as the person who traveled across North America, planting apple orchards.

K

Kaboi (kah boy) was a very wise man in a Carajá myth. He helped his people find their way from their underground home to the surface of the earth.

Kewawkwuí (kay wow kwoo) were a group of powerful, frightening giants and magicians in the myths of Algonquian Native American people.

Kigbo (keeg boh) was a stubborn man in a Yoruba myth of Africa. His stubbornness got him into trouble with spirits.

Kodoyanpe (koh doh yahn pay) was a good god in the myths of the Maidu and some other Native American people. He was the brother of the evil god Coyote.

Kuang Zi Lian (kwahng dsee lee ehm) in a Taoist myth of China was a very rich, greedy farmer who was punished by one of the Eight Immortals.

Kui in Chinese myths was an ugly, brilliant scholar who became God of Examinations.

Kvasir (KVAH sihr) in Norse myths was the wisest of all the gods in Asgard.

L

Lancelot (lan suh laht) in British and Welsh legends was King Arthur's friend and greatest knight. He was secretly in love with Guinevere.

Lao Zi (low dzuh) was the man who founded the Chinese religion of Taoism. He wrote down the Taoist beliefs in a book, the *Tao Te Ching*.

Li Xuan (lee shwahn) was one of the Eight Immortals in ancient Chinese myths.

Light (lyt) was a child of Amma, the creator of the world, in a myth of the Dogon people of Africa.

Lizard (LIHZ urd) was an animal prince in an Alur myth of Africa. He was certain that he, and not his brother, Frog, would inherit the throne of their father.

Llew Llaw Gyffes (LE yoo HLA yoo GUHF ehs), also Lleu Law Gyffes, was a hero in Welsh myths who had many adventures. His mother was Arianrod and his father was Gwydion.

Loki (LOH kee) in Norse myths was a master trickster. His friends were Odin and Thor. Loki was half giant and half god, and could be funny and also cruel. He caused the death of Balder.

Lord of Heaven was the chief god in some ancient Chinese myths.

Lug (luk) in Irish myths was the Immortal High King of Ireland, Master of All Arts.

M

Maira-Monan (mah ee rah moh nahn) was the most powerful son of Irin-Mage in Tupinambá myths. He was destroyed by people who were afraid of his powers.

Manco Capac (mahn kih kah pahk) in Inca myths was the founder of the Inca people. He was one of four brothers and four sisters who led the Inca to their homeland.

Manitou (MAN ih toh) was the greatest and most powerful of all gods in Native American myths of the Iroquois people.

Math (mohth) in Welsh myths was a magician who ruled the Welsh kingdom of Gwynedd.

Michabo (mee chah boh) in the myths of Algonquian Native American people was the Great Hare, who taught people to hunt and brought them luck. He was a son of West Wind.

Monan (moh nahn) was the creator in Tupinambá myths.

Monkey (MUNG kee) is the hero of many Chinese stories. The most cunning of all monkeys, he became the king of monkeys and caused great troubles for the gods.

N

Nanook (na NOOK) was the white bear in myths of the Inuit people.

Naoise (NEE see) in Irish myths was Conchobar's nephew and the lover of Deirdre. He was the son of Usnech and brother of Ardan and Ainle.

Nekumonta (neh koo mohn tah) in Native American myths of the Iroquois people was a person whose goodness helped him save his people from a terrible sickness.

Nü Wa (nyuh wah) in a Chinese myth was a girl who, with her brother, Fu Xi, freed the Thunder God and was rewarded. Her name means Gourd Girl.

Nuada (NOO uh thuh) in Irish myths was King of the Tuatha Dé Danann, the rulers of all Ireland. He had a silver hand.

O

Odin (OH dihn), also called Woden, in Norse myths was the chief of all the gods and a brave warrior. He had only one eye. He was the husband of Frigga and father of many of the gods. His two advisers were the ravens Hugin and Munin.

Odysseus (oh DIHS ee uhs) was a Greek hero who fought in the Trojan War. The poet Homer wrote of his many adventures.

Oedipus (ED uh puhs) was a tragic hero in Greek myths. He unknowingly killed his own father and married his mother.

Olodumare (oh loh doo mah ray) was the supreme god in Yoruba myths of Africa.

Olokun (oh loh koon) was the god of water and giver of life in Yoruba myths of Africa. He challenged Olodumare for the right to rule.

Orpheus (AWR fee uhs) in Greek myths was famed for his music. He followed his wife, Euridice, to the kingdom of the dead to plead for her life.

Osiris (oh SY rihs) in ancient Egypt was the ruler of the dead in the kingdom of the West. He was the brother and husband of Isis and the father of Horus.

P

Pamola (pah moh lah) in the myths of Algonquian Native American people was an evil spirit of the night.

Pan Gu (pahn goo) in Chinese myths was the giant who was the first living being.

Pandora (pan DAWR uh) in ancient Greek myths was the first woman.

Paris (PAR ihs) was a real person, a hero from the city of Troy. He captured Helen, the queen of a Greek kingdom, and took her to Troy.

Paul Bunyan (pawl BUHN yuhn) was a tremendously strong giant lumberjack in North American myths.

Perseus (PUR see uhs) was a human hero in myths of ancient Greece. His most famous adventure was killing Medusa, a creature who turned anyone who looked at her to stone.

Poseidon (puh SY duhn) was the god of the sea in myths of ancient Greece. He carried a three-pronged spear called a trident to make storms and control the waves. The Romans called him Neptune.

Prometheus (pruh MEE thee uhs) was the cleverest of the gods in Greek myths. He was a friend to humankind.

Q

Queen Mother of the West was a goddess in Chinese myths.

R

Ra (rah), sometimes Re (ray), was the sun god of ancient Egypt. He was often shown with the head of a hawk. Re became the most important god. Other gods were sometimes combined with him and had Ra added to their names.

Ran (rahn) was the goddess of the sea in Norse myths. She pulled sailors from their boats in a large net and dragged them underwater.

Red Jacket in Chinese myths was an assistant to Wen Chang, the god of literature. His job was to help students who hadn't worked very hard.

S

Sekhmet (SEHK meht) in ancient Egypt was a blood-thirsty goddess with the head of a lioness. She was the daughter of Ra and the sister of Bastet and Hathor.

Setanta in Irish myths was Cuchulain's name before he killed the hound of Culan.

Seth (set), sometimes Set, in ancient Egypt was the god of chaos and confusion, who fought Horus to rule Egypt. He was the evil son of Geb and Nut.

Shanewis (shah nay wihs) in Native American myths of the Iroquois people was the wife of Nekumonta.

Shu (shoo) in ancient Egypt was the father of the sky goddess Nut. He held Nut above Geb, the Earth, to keep the two apart.

Sinchi Roca was the second emperor of the Inca. According to legend, he was the son of Ayar Manco (later known as Manco Capac) and his sister Mama Ocllo.

Skirnir (SKEER nihr) in Norse myths was a brave, faithful servant of the god Frey.

Sphinx (sfihngks) in Greek myths was a creature that was half lion and half woman, with eagle wings. It killed anyone who failed to answer its riddle.

T

Tefnut (TEHF noot) was the moon goddess in ancient Egypt. She was the sister and wife of Shu and the mother of Nut and Geb.

Theseus (THEE see uhs) was a human hero in myths of ancient Greece. He killed the Minotaur, a half-human, half-bull creature, and freed its victims.

Thor (thawr) was the god of thunder in Norse myths. He crossed the skies in a chariot pulled by goats and had a hammer, Mjollnir, and a belt, Meginjardir.

Thunder God (THUN dur gahd) in Chinese myths was the god of thunder and rain. He got his power from water and was powerless if he could not drink.

Tsui'goab (tsoo ee goh ahb) was the god of rain in myths of the Khoi people of Africa. He was a human who became a god after he fought to save his people.

Tupan (too pahn) was the spirit of thunder and lightning in Inca myths.

Tyr (tihr) was the god of war in Norse myths. He was the bravest god and was honorable and true, as well. He had just one hand.

U

Utgard-Loki (OOT gahrd LOH kee) in Norse myths was the clever, crafty giant king of Utgard. He once disguised himself as a giant called Skrymir to teach Thor a lesson.

W

Water God (WAW tur gahd) in Chinese myths was a god who sent rain and caused floods.

Wen Chang (wehn chuhng) in Chinese myths was the god of literature. His assistants were Kui and Red Jacket.

Wu (woo) was a lowly courtier in a Chinese myth who fell in love with a princess.

X

Xi He (shee heh) in Chinese myths was the goddess wife of Di Jun, the god of the eastern sky.

Xiwangmu (shee wahng moo) in Chinese myths was the owner of the Garden of Immortal Peaches.

Xuan Zang (shwahn dsahng), also called Tripitaka, was a real person, a Chinese Buddhist monk who traveled to India to gather copies of religious writings. Legends about him tell that Monkey was his traveling companion.

Y

Yan Wang (yahn wahng) was the god of the dead and judge of the first court of the Underworld in Chinese myths. He was helper to Di Zang Wang.

Yao (yow) was a virtuous emperor in Chinese myths. Because Yao lived simply and was a good leader, Yi the Archer was sent to help him.

Yi (yee) was an archer in Chinese myths who was sent by Di Jun to save the earth, in answer to Yao's prayers.

Z

Zeus (zoos) in ancient Greece was the king of gods and the god of thunder and lightning. The Romans called him Jupiter.

Zhao Shen Xiao (zhow shehn shi ow) in Chinese myths was a good magistrate, or official, who arrested the greedy merchant Kuang Zi Lian.

MYTHS AND LEGENDS GLOSSARY

This is a cumulative glossary of some important places and terms found in all eight volumes of the **World Book Myths and Legends** series.

A

Alfheim (AHLF hym) in Norse myth was the home of the light elves.

Asgard (AS gahrd) in Norse myths was the home of the warrior gods who were called the Aesir. It was connected to the earth by a rainbow bridge.

Augean (aw JEE uhn) stables were stables that the Greek hero Heracles had to clean as one of his twelve labors. He made the waters of two rivers flow through the stables and wash away the filth.

Avalon (AV uh lahn) in British legends was the island where King Arthur was carried after he died in battle. The legend says he will rise again to lead Britain.

B

Bard (bahrd) was a Celtic poet and singer in ancient times. A bard entertained people by making up and singing poems about brave deeds.

Battle of the Alamo (AL uh moh) was a battle between Texas settlers and Mexican forces when Texas was fighting for independence from Mexico. It took place at the Alamo, a fort in San Antonio, in 1836.

Bifrost (BEE fruhst) in Norse myths was a rainbow bridge that connected Asgard with the world of people.

Black Land in ancient Egypt was the area of fertile soil around the banks of the River Nile. Most people lived there.

Brer Rabbit (brair RAB iht) myths are African American stories about a rabbit who played tricks on his friends. The stories grew out of animal myths from Africa.

C

Canoe Mountain in a Maidu myth of North America was the mountain on which the evil Coyote took refuge from a flood sent to drown him.

Changeling (CHAYNG lihng) in Celtic myths was a fairy child who had been swapped with a human baby at birth. Changelings were usually lazy and clumsy.

Confucianism (kuhn FYOO shuhn IHZ uhm) is a Chinese way of life and religion. It is based on the teachings of Confucius, also known as Kong Fu Zi, and is more than 2,000 years old.

Creation myths

Creation myths (kree AY shuhn mihths) are myths that tell how the world began.

D

Dwarfs (dwawrfs) in Norse myths were small people of great power. They were skilled at making tools and weapons.

F

Fairies (FAIR eez) in Celtic myths were called the Little People. They are especially common in Irish legends, where they are called leprechauns.

Fomors (FOH wawrz) in Irish myths were hideous giants who invaded Ireland and were fought by Lug.

G

Giants (JY uhnts) in Norse myths were huge people who had great strength and great powers. They often struggled with the warrior gods of Asgard.

Gnome (nohm) was a small, odd-looking person in the myths of many civilizations. In Inca myths, for example, gnomes were tiny people with very big beards.

Golden Apples of the Hesperides (heh SPEHR uh deez) were apples of gold in a garden that only the Greek gods could enter. They were collected by the hero Heracles as one of his twelve labors.

Golden fleece was the fleece of a ram that the Greek hero Jason won after many adventures with his ship, Argo, and his companion sailors, the Argonauts.

Green Knoll (nohl) was the home of the Little People, or fairies, in Irish and Scottish myths.

J

Jotunheim (YUR toon hym) in Norse myths was the land of the giants.

L

Lion men in myths of Africa were humans who can turn themselves into lions.

Little People in Celtic legends and folk tales are fairies. They are often fine sword makers and blacksmiths.

M

Machu Picchu (MAH choo PEE choo) is the ruins of an ancient city built by the Inca in the Andes Mountains of Peru.

Medecolin (may day coh leen) were a tribe of evil sorcerers in the myths of Algonquian Native American people.

Medicine (MEHD uh sihn) **man** is a wise man or shaman who has special powers. Medicine men also appear as beings with special powers in myths of Africa and North and South America. Also see **Shaman.**

Midgard (MIHD gahrd) in Norse myths was the world of people.

Muspell (MOOS pehl) in Norse myths was part of the Underworld. It was a place of fire.

N

Nidavellir in Norse myths was the land of the dwarfs.

Niflheim in Norse myths was part of the Underworld. It included Hel, the kingdom of the dead.

Nirvana (nur VAH nuh) in the religion of Buddhism is a state of happiness that people find when they have freed themselves from wanting things. People who reach Nirvana no longer have to be reborn.

O

Oracle (AWRR uh kuhl) in ancient Greece was a sacred place served by people who could foretell the future. Greeks journeyed there to ask questions about their fortunes. Also see **Soothsayer.**

P

Pacariqtambo (pahk kah ree TAHM boh) in Inca myths was a place of three caves from which the first people stepped out into the world. It is also called Paccari Tampu.

Poppykettle was a clay kettle made for brewing poppy-seed tea. In an Inca myth, a poppykettle was used for a boat.

Prophecy (PRAH feh see) is a prediction made by some-one who foretells the future.

R

Ragnarok (RAHG nah ruhk) in Norse myths was the final battle of good and evil, in which the giants would fight against the gods of Asgard.

S

Sahara (sah HAH rah) is a vast desert that covers much of northern Africa.

Seriema was a bird in a Carajá myth of South America whose call led the first people to try to find their way from underground to the surface of the earth.

Shaman (SHAH muhn) can be a real person, a medicine man or wise person who knows the secrets of nature. Shamans also appear as beings with special powers in some myths of North and South America. Also see **Medicine man.**

Soothsayer (sooth SAY ur) in ancient Greece was some-one who could see into the future. Also see **Oracle.**

Svartalfheim (SVAHRT uhl hym) in Norse myths was the home of the dark elves.

T

Tar Baby was a sticky doll made of tar used to trap Brer Rabbit, a tricky rabbit in African American folk tales.

Tara (TAH rah) in Irish myths was the high seat, or ruling place, of the Irish kings.

Trickster (TRIHK stur) **animals** are clever ones that appear in many myths of North America, South America, and Africa.

Trojan horse. See **Wooden horse of Troy.**

Tuatha dè Danann (THOO uh huh day DUH nuhn) were the people of the goddess Danu. Later they were known as gods of Ireland themselves.

V

Vanaheim (VAH nah hym) in Norse myths was the home of the fertility gods.

W

Wadjet eye was a symbol used by the people of ancient Egypt. It stood for the eye of the gods Ra and Horus and was supposed to bring luck.

Wheel of Transmigration (tranz my GRAY shuhn) in the religion of Buddhism is the wheel people's souls reach after they die. From there they are sent back to earth to be born into a higher or lower life.

Wooden horse of Troy was a giant wooden horse built by the Greeks during the Trojan War. The Greeks hid soldiers in the horse's belly and left the horse for the Trojans to find.

Y

Yang (yang) is the male quality of light, sun, heat, and dryness in Chinese beliefs. Yang struggles with Yin for control of things.

Yatkot was a magical tree in an African myth of the Alur people.

Yggdrasil (IHG drah sihl) in Norse myths was a mighty tree that held all three worlds together and reached up into the stars.

Yin (yihn) is the female quality of shadow, moon, cold, and water in Chinese beliefs. Yin struggles with Yang for control of things.

CUMULATIVE INDEX

This is an alphabetical list of important topics covered in all eight volumes of the **World Book Myths and Legends** series. Next to each entry is at least one pair of numbers separated by a slash mark (/). For example, the entry for Argentina is "**Argentina 8/4**". The first number tells you what volume to look in for information. The second number tells you what page you should turn to in that volume. Sometimes a topic appears in more than one place. When it does, additional volume and page numbers are given. Here's a reminder of the volume numbers and titles: 1, *African Myths and Legends*; 2, *Ancient Egyptian Myths and Legends*; 3, *Ancient Greek Myths and Legends*; 4, *Celtic Myths and Legends*; 5, *Chinese Myths and Legends*; 6, *Norse Myths and Legends*; 7, *North American Myths and Legends*; 8, *South American Myths and Legends*.

Oedipus, a tragic hero 3/5, 3/43–47
Olodumare, the supreme god 1/7–11
Olokun, god of the sea 1/6–11
Olympus, Mount, home of the gods 3/4, 3/19, 3/23, 3/25, 3/29
oracles 3/14, 3/44, 3/46
Orpheus, husband of Eurydice 3/5, 3/33
Osiris, ruler of the dead 2/5
  murder of 2/7–11
  search for 2/13–17

P

Pacariqtambo, the place of origin 8/31, 8/33, 8/35
Pamola, evil spirit of the night 7/17
Pan Gu, the first living being 5/43
Pandora, the first woman 3/5, 3/43
papyrus 2/3
Paris, a Trojan hero 3/5, 3/34–35
Pasiphaë, wife of King Minos 3/14
Pegasus, the winged horse 3/22–23
Periboea, queen of Corinth 3/44, 3/46
Persephone, wife of Hades 3/33
Perseus, a hero 3/4, 3/9, 3/22
Peru 8/2, 8/4, 8/31, 8/37
pharaohs, rulers of Egypt 2/2, 2/31–35
Phineus, soothsayer king of Thrace 3/38–39
Poetic Edda, a collection of stories 6/2–3
Polybus, king of Corinth 3/44, 3/46
Polyphemus, the Cyclops 3/31–32
Poppykettle, a sailing vessel 8/37, 8/39–41
Poseidon, god of the sea 3/4, 3/13, 3/14, 3/31
Priam, king of Troy 3/34
Proitos, king of Argos 3/22, 3/23
Prometheus, a god 3/4, 3/19, 3/28
Prose Edda, a collection of stories 6/2
pyramids of Egypt 2/2

Q

Queen Mother of the West, a goddess 5/16

R

Ra, the sun god 2/2, 2/4, 2/5, 2/7, 2/17, 2/20
  destruction of humankind 2/25–29
  secret name 2/43–47
Ragnarok, final battle 6/4, 6/23, 6/27, 6/47
Raleigh, Sir Walter, an English explorer 8/5
Ran, goddess of the sea 6/5
  net used by Loki 6/15, 6/44
Ratatosk, a squirrel 6/3
Red Jacket, assistant to the God of Literature 5/40–41
Regin, a dwarf 6/5, 6/14, 6/16
religion 1/3, 5/4–5, 8/2, 8/25
Rhampsinitus, a rich pharaoh 2/31–35
Ringhorn, a longboat 6/41, 6/42
Romans, ancient 3/3

S

Sahara 1/2
sailor myth 2/37–41
savanna 8/19, 8/20
secret name of Ra 2/43–47
Sekhmet, daughter of Ra 2/5
seriema, a bird 8/19, 8/20, 8/21, 8/23
serpents 6/10–11, 6/46–47
Seth, god of chaos 2/5, 2/8–11, 2/16–17, 2/19–23
shamans 7/4, 7/44–45, 8/27, 8/28
Shanewis, wife of Nekumonta 7/10–15
Sherente, a South American people 8/3, 8/43–47
shipwreck myth 2/37–41
Shu, father of Nut 2/5, 2/19
Sigurd, a dwarf 6/17
Signy, goddess wife of Loki 6/47
silk 5/3
Sinchi Roca, second emperor of the Inca 8/34, 8/35
Sioux, a North American people 7/25
Skadi, a giantess 6/46
Skirnir, a servant 6/5, 6/21–22, 6/25–27
slavery 1/5, 7/2, 7/3, 7/39, 7/40–41
snake meat 7/25
snake myths 2/38–41, 2/44–46
Snorri Sturluson, Icelandic author 6/2–3
soothsayers 3/7, 3/38–39, 3/46, 3/47
souls, land of the 1/6–7
South African myth 1/13–17
South American peoples 8/2–5
  see also under individual groups, e.g., **Inca; Kayapó; Sherente**
Spanish conquest of South America 8/5, 8/37, 8/38
Sphinx, half lion, half woman 3/45–46
spirit of the mountain 1/37–38, 1/40
stars, the creation of 8/7–11
Stymphalian Birds 3/27
sun gods 2/4, 8/5
  see also **Ra**
Svartalfheim, land of dark elves 6/3
Symplegades Rocks 3/38, 3/39

T

Talos, nephew of Daedalus 3/20–21
tamarisk tree 2/14, 2/15
Taoism 5/5, 5/31–35
Tar Baby see **Brer Rabbit and the Tar Baby**
Tartarus, the Underworld 3/29, 3/33
Tata, a terrible fire from heaven 8/26
Tefnut, a moon goddess 2/5
Teiresias, a soothsayer 3/46, 3/47
Theseus, a hero 3/4, 3/15–17, 3/20
Thialfi, a servant 6/7, 6/8, 6/10
Thor, god of thunder 6/4, 6/36, 6/37, 6/38
  downfall of Loki 6/44–47
  in the land of giants 6/7–11
  stolen hammer myth 6/29–33
Thrym, a giant 6/30–33
Thunder God 5/7–10
Tree of Life 6/3
trickster animals 1/5, 8/4

ISBN(set): 0-7166-2613-6
African Myths and Legends
ISBN: 0-7166-2605-5
LC: 2001026492
Ancient Egyptian Myths and Legends
ISBN: 0-7166-2606-3
LC: 2001026501
Ancient Greek Myths and Legends
ISBN: 0-7166-2607-1
LC: 2001035959
Celtic Myths and Legends
ISBN: 0-7166-2608-X
LC: 2001026496
Chinese Myths and Legends
ISBN: 0-7166-2609-8
LC: 2001026489
Norse Myths and Legends
ISBN: 0-7166-2610-1
LC: 2001026488
North American Myths and Legends
ISBN: 0-7166-2611-X
LC: 2001026490
South American Myths and Legends
ISBN: 0-7166-2612-8
LC: 2001026491

For information on other World Book products, visit our Web site at www.worldbook.com or call 1-800-WORLDBK (967-5325).

For information on sales to schools and libraries, call 1-800-975-3250.

Cover background illustration by Paul Perreault

World Book, Inc.
233 North Michigan Avenue
Chicago, IL 60601

Printed in the United States of America
1 2 3 4 5 6 7 8 9 10 10 09 08 07 06 05 04 03 02 01